THE VERITAS BOOK OF BLESSINGS FOR ALL OCCASIONS

THE VERITAS
BOOK OF BLESSINGS
FOR ALL OCCASIONS

First published 2013 by
Veritas Publications
7–8 Lower Abbey Street
Dublin 1
publications@veritas.ie
www.veritas.ie

Edited by Columba McCann osb

Printed with ecclesiastical approval

ISBN 978 1 84730 517 6

10 9 8 7 6 5 4 3 2 1

Acknowledgements

Excerpts from the English translation of the *Book of Blessings* © 1989, International Committee on English in the Liturgy, Inc. (ICEL). Excerpts from *The Veritas Book of Blessing Prayers* © 1989, Veritas Publications. Excerpts from *Pastoral Care of the Sick: Rights of Anointing and Viaticum* © 1982, ICEL. Excerpts from the *Order of Christian Funerals* © 1985, ICEL. Excerpts from the *Jerusalem Bible*, published and copyright 1985 by Darton, Longman and Todd Ltd and Doubleday & Co. Inc.

A catalogue record for this book is available from the British Library.

Designed by Colette Dower, Veritas Publications
Printed in the Republic of Ireland by Speciality Printing, Dublin

Veritas books are printed on paper made from the wood pulp of managed forests. For every tree felled, at least one tree is planted, thereby renewing natural resources.

CONTENTS

INTRODUCTION

HOW THIS BOOK WAS WRITTEN

This book is a compilation of blessings taken mostly from the *Book of Blessings* and adapted for local use. Such adaptation is both permitted and encouraged. The Latin text of the *Book of Blessings* (*De Benedictionibus*) was published in 1984 and, while an English translation of this text was still unavailable, the *Veritas Book of Blessing Prayers* was published as an interim and supplementary resource. This volume was put together with the assistance of thirty-one contributors with experience in a wide range of pastoral circumstances. The wide, locally-based experience which informed this publication reflected particular pastoral needs as identified in Ireland and provided a language to address those needs. It also reflected a realistic assessment of the size of book needed and the length of texts to be provided. An English translation of *De Benedictionibus* was prepared by the International Commission on English in the Liturgy (ICEL) and published in 1989 in a volume running to seven hundred and ninety-nine pages. In the present publication, the interim Veritas publication was used as a guide to identify those situations for which a blessing text was required. The most suitable blessings in the ICEL text were then selected and adapted for local use. Some pastoral situations identified in Ireland have no explicit counterpart in the ICEL text. In these instances a more generic blessing prayer was used from the ICEL text, supplemented by intercessions reflecting the pastoral needs and the language preferred in the Irish volume. There were still some other instances where no blessing prayer in the ICEL text seemed adequate to the pastoral situation. Here the solution was to provide texts either from other liturgical books or from the earlier *Veritas Book of Blessing Prayers*, sometimes with minor adjustments. These are found under the heading Additional Prayers. It goes without saying that, in many pastoral situations, further adaptation of the texts given in this volume will be required. It should also be mentioned that some texts taken from the *Book of Blessings*, for example the commissioning of Extraordinary Ministers of Holy Communion, are not to be found in the original Latin *De Benedictionibus*, but were produced for use in the USA and approved for use by the United States Conference of Catholic Bishops.

SOME IMPORTANT RESOURCES FOR ADDITIONAL TEXTS

The *Book of Blessings*, from which most of the texts in this volume are taken, remains an important resource for additional texts. Mention should also be made of *The Pastoral Care of the Sick*, the basic text for liturgical celebrations for the sick, from which some of the prayers were also taken. The prayers for the dead were taken from the *Order of Christian Funerals*, which provides resources not only for the funeral Mass and burial, but also for a variety of other ritual moments surrounding the death of a Christian. A most helpful collection of additional scripture readings for use in a variety of situations is to be found in volume three of the *Lectionary*, which provides texts for Ritual Masses and Masses for Various Needs and Occasions. Many of these texts will suit comparable liturgical celebrations outside Mass. The Collects for Masses for Special Needs and Occasions given in the *Roman Missal* are another useful source for prayer texts.

THE IMPORTANCE OF GOD'S WORD IN THE LITURGICAL CELEBRATION OF GOD'S BLESSING

While liturgical blessings normally include a dynamic of petition in which we invoke God's saving help, they are always, in the first instance, a moment in which we are addressed by God's love. A liturgical blessing is not an attempt on our part to change God, but a graced moment which opens us up to being changed by God. In this context the hearing of God's word assumes particular importance, and this is why scriptural readings are rarely omitted. This becomes an even more important consideration in those pastoral situations where the possibility of a superstitious or quasi-magical approach to blessings is anticipated.

SUGGESTIONS FOR A RICH LITURGICAL CELEBRATION OF GOD'S BLESSING

In order to keep this volume to a manageable size, the texts and descriptions of many of the rites are fairly short. What is given often represents little more than the minimum required for the celebration. Liturgical celebrations by their nature best include a number of elements: a gathering of members of the Christian community, the proclamation of the word of God, involvement of a variety of ministers, intercession, singing and symbolic gesture of some kind. Thus there will be many instances when a fuller celebration is called for. Those planning the celebration may consider adding in some or all of the elements listed below.

- Songs at the beginning and the end of the celebration (see examples pp. 18–19)
- A liturgical greeting after the Sign of the Cross (see examples p. 20)
- A responsorial psalm or a suitable song after the reading from sacred scripture (see examples pp. 21–22)
- A brief explanation of the biblical text in its liturgical context.
- Some intercessions before the Prayer of Blessing and, where appropriate, the Lord's Prayer
- A final blessing (see examples pp. 23–25)

SOME WELL-KNOWN SONGS

The following songs are either well-known or easily learnt for use during the celebration of various blessings given in this book.

Abbreviations
VH = *Veritas Hymnal*
AA = *Alleluia Amen*
IC = *In Caelo*

General
Be Thou My Vision (VH)
Christ Be Beside Me (VH)
Spirit of the Living God
The King of Love My Shepherd Is (VH)
The Lord is My Shepherd (VH)
May Your Love Be Upon Us, O Lord (AA)
Love is His Word (VH)

Advent
O Come Emmanuel (VH)

Christmas
Silent Night (VH)
Angels We Have Heard on High (VH)

Easter
Come Christians All (VH)
Jesus Christ is Risen Today (VH)
Seinn Ailliluia (IC)

Harvest
Ag Críost an Síol (VH)

Healing
Lay Your Hands Gently Upon Us (Carey Landry)

Praise and Thanksgiving
The Lourdes Magnificat (AA)
Praise My Soul the King of Heaven (VH)

Our Lady
When Creation Was Begun (VH)
As I Kneel Before You

Songs Whose Tunes Are Familiar Among Most Christian Denominations
All People That On Earth Do Dwell (VH)
Be Thou My Vision (VH)
Praise My Soul the King of Heaven (VH)
The King of Love My Shepherd Is (VH)

SOME LITURGICAL GREETINGS

In order to facilitate participation, ordained ministers are advised to use greetings which are already familiar to the people, for example, 'The Lord be with you' or 'The grace of our Lord Jesus Christ, and the love of God and the communion of the Holy Spirit be with you all.'

The following greetings for use by lay ministers are taken from the *Book of Blessings*:

Our help is in the name of the Lord.
R Who made heaven and earth.

And

Blessed be the name of the Lord.
R Now and for ever.

SOME RESPONSORIAL PSALMS

I

R To you, O Lord, I lift up my soul.

Lord, make me know your ways,
Lord, teach me your paths,
Make me walk in your truth, and teach me:
for you are God my saviour. R

The Lord is good and upright.
He shows the path to those who stray,
he guides the humble in the right path;
he teaches his way to the poor. R

His ways are faithfulness and love
for those who keep his covenant and will.
The Lord's friendship is for those who revere him;
to them he reveals his covenant. R

II

R We are his people, the sheep of his flock.

Cry out with joy to the Lord, all the earth.
Serve the Lord with gladness.
Come before him, singing for joy. R

Know that he, the Lord, is God.
He made us, we belong to him,
we are his people, the sheep of his flock. R

Indeed, how good is the Lord,
eternal his merciful love.
He is faithful from age to age. R

III

R The Lord is compassion and love.

My, soul, give thanks to the Lord,
all my being, bless his holy name.
My soul, give thanks to the Lord
and never forget all his blessings. R

It is he who forgives all your guilt,
who heals every one of your ills,
who redeems your life from the grave,
who crowns you with love and compassion. R

The Lord is compassion and love,
slow to anger and rich in mercy.
He does not treat us according to our sins
nor repay us according to our faults. R

As far as the east is from the west
so far does he remove our sins.
As a father has compassion on his sons,
the Lord has pity on those who fear him. R

SOME FINAL BLESSINGS FOR USE BY PRIESTS AND DEACONS

Ordained ministers may conclude using a simple blessing as at the conclusion of Mass. The following solemn blessings are also suitable for many occasions:

I

May the Lord bless you and keep you.
R Amen.

May his face shine upon you, and be gracious to you.
R Amen.

May he look upon you with kindness, and give you his peace.
R Amen.

May almighty God bless you, the Father, and the Son, ✠ and the Holy Spirit.
R Amen.

II

May the peace of God
which is beyond all understanding
keep your hearts and minds
in the knowledge and love of God
and of his Son, our Lord Jesus Christ.
R Amen.

May almighty God bless you, the Father, and the Son, ✠ and the Holy Spirit.
R Amen.

May the God of all grace,
who has called you to his eternal glory in Christ,
confirm you and make you strong and sure in your
faith.
R Amen.

May almighty God bless you, the Father, and the Son,
✠ and the Holy Spirit.
R Amen.

A broader selection of solemn blessings is available in
the *Roman Missal*.

SOME FINAL BLESSINGS
FOR USE BY LAY MINISTERS

Lay ministers may conclude the rites by signing themselves with the sign of the cross while saying the appropriate prayer of blessing. The following are taken from the *Book of Blessings*:

May God bless us with his mercy,
strengthen us with his love,
and enable us to walk in charity and peace.
R Amen.

May our all-merciful God, Father, Son, and Holy Spirit,
bless us and embrace us in love for ever.
R Amen.

May the Lord bless us,
protect us from all evil,
and bring us to everlasting life.
R Amen.

May God give us peace in our sorrow,
consolation in our grief,
and strength to accept his will in all things.
R Amen.

May the God of hope fill you with every joy in believing.
May the peace of Christ abound in your hearts.
May the Holy Spirit enrich you with his gifts,
now and for ever.
R Amen.

BLESSINGS OF PERSONS

BLESSINGS OF FAMILIES
AND FAMILY MEMBERS

BLESSING OF A FAMILY[1]
In the name of the Father and of the Son and of the Holy Spirit.
R Amen.

One of those present or the minister reads a text of sacred scripture, for example:

Brothers and sisters, listen to the words of the first letter of Paul to the Corinthians 13:4-7:

Love is always patient and kind; love is never jealous; love is not boastful or conceited, it is never rude or selfish, it does not take offence, and is not resentful. Love takes no pleasure in other people's sins but delights in the truth; it is always ready to excuse, to trust, to hope, and to endure whatever comes.

Love never comes to an end.

Some intercessions, composed specially for the occasion, may follow.

The minister invites all present to sing or say the Lord's Prayer.

All: Our Father …

---

[1] Adapted from the *Book of Blessings*, n. 46ff

The minister says the prayer of blessing:

We bless your name, O Lord,
for sending your own incarnate Son
to become part of a family,
so that, as he lived its life,
he would experience its worries and its joys.

We ask you, Lord,
to protect and watch over this family,
so that in the strength of your grace
its members may enjoy prosperity,
possess the priceless gift of your peace,
and, as the Church alive in the home,
bear witness in this world to your glory.

Through Christ our Lord.
R Amen.

As circumstances suggest, the minister in silence may sprinkle the family with holy water.

The minister concludes the rite by saying:

May the Lord Jesus,
who lived with his holy family in Nazareth,
dwell also with your family,
keep it from all evil,
and make all of you one in heart and mind.
R Amen.

BLESSING OF A MARRIED COUPLE ON THE ANNIVERSARY OF MARRIAGE[2]

Blessing Within Mass

After the homily the celebrant invites the couple to pray in silence. He may bless their rings, saying:

Lord,
bless ✠ and consecrate the love which N. and N. have for one another.
May these rings be a symbol
of their true faith in each other
and always remind them of their love.
Through Christ our Lord.
R Amen.

The general intercessions follow. Through the intentions proposed, those present could pray for God's blessing on the couple, the gift of fidelity, serenity in Christ through good times and bad, as well as the witness of all married couples to Christian living. The intercessions may conclude with the following prayer:

O God, the life of the family is founded on the plan of your own providence.
In your mercy receive the prayers of your servants.
Grant that by imitating the Holy Family they may reach the joys of your home and together praise you for ever.
Through Christ our Lord.
R Amen.

---

[2] Adapted from the *Book of Blessings*, n. 94ff

Prayer of Blessing

After the Lord's prayer, and omitting the embolism 'Deliver us', the celebrant faces the couple and, with hands outstretched, says:

Lord God and Creator,
we bless and praise your name.
In the beginning you made man and woman,
so that they might enter a communion of life and love.
You likewise blessed the union of N. with N.,
so that they might reflect the union of Christ with his Church:
look with kindness on them today.
Amid the joys and struggles of their life
you have preserved the union between them;
renew their marriage covenant,
increase your love in them,
and strengthen their bond of peace,
so that (surrounded by their children)
they may always rejoice in the gift of your blessing.
Through Christ our Lord.
R Amen.

Blessing Outside Mass

In the name of the Father and of the Son and of the Holy Spirit.
R Amen.

One of those present or the minister reads a text of sacred scripture, for example, John 15:9-11:

Jesus said, 'Remain in my love. If you keep my commandments you will remain in my love, just as I have kept my Father's commandments and remain in

his love. I have told you this so that my own joy might
be in you and your joy be complete.'

The minister says the prayer of blessing:

Lord God and Creator,
we bless and praise your name.
In the beginning you made man and woman,
so that they might enter a communion of life and love.
You likewise blessed the union of N. with N.,
so that they might reflect the union of Christ with his
Church:
look with kindness on them today.
Amid the joys and struggles of their life
you have preserved the union between them;
renew their marriage covenant,
increase your love in them,
and strengthen their bond of peace,
so that (surrounded by their children)
they may always rejoice in the gift of your blessing.

Through Christ our Lord.
R Amen.

BLESSING OF A MARRIED COUPLE ON OTHER OCCASIONS[3]

Blessing Within Mass

After the homily the celebrant invites the couple to pray in silence and to renew before God their marriage commitment to one another.

The general intercessions follow. The following prayer of blessing concludes the intercessions:

Almighty and eternal God,
you have so exalted the unbreakable bond of marriage
that it has become the sacramental sign
of your Son's union with the Church as his spouse.

Look with favour on N. and N., whom you have united in marriage,
as they ask for your help
and the protection of the Virgin Mary.
They pray that in good times and in bad
they will grow in love for each other;
that they will resolve to be of one heart
in the bond of peace.

Lord, in their struggles let them rejoice
that you are near to help them;
in their needs let them know
that you are there to rescue them;
in their joys let them see
that you are the source and completion of every happiness.

Through Christ our Lord.
R Amen.

---

[3] Adapted from the *Book of Blessing*, n. 110ff

Blessing Outside Mass

In the name of the Father and of the Son and of the Holy Spirit.

R Amen.

One of those present or the minister reads a text of sacred scripture, for example, John 15:9-11:

Jesus said, 'Remain in my love. If you keep my commandments you will remain in my love, just as I have kept my Father's commandments and remain in his love. I have told you this so that my own joy might be in you and your joy be complete.'

The minister says the prayer of blessing as at Mass above.

BLESSING OF CHILDREN
BY THEIR PARENTS

In the name of the Father and of the Son and of the Holy Spirit.

R Amen.

One of those present reads a text of sacred scripture, for example:

Brothers and sisters, listen to the words of the holy gospel according to Matthew 19:13-15:

People brought little children to him, for him to lay his hands on them and say a prayer. The disciples turned them away, but Jesus said, 'Let the children alone, and do not stop them coming to me; for it is to such as these that the kingdom of heaven belongs.' Then he laid his hands on them and went on his way.

As circumstances suggest, the parents may trace the sign of the cross on their children's forehead; they then say the prayer of blessing:

Father,
inexhaustible source of life and author of all good,
we bless you and we thank you
for brightening our communion of love by your gift of children.
Grant that our children/child will find in the life of this family such inspiration

---

[4] Adapted from the *Book of Blessings*, n. 179ff

that they/he/she will strive always for what is right
and good
and one day, by your grace,
reach their/his/her home in heaven.
Through Christ our Lord.
R Amen.

A minister who is not a parent of the children says the
following prayer of blessing:

Lord Jesus Christ,
you loved children so much that you said
'Whoever welcomes a child welcomes me.'
Hear our prayers and, with your unfailing protection,
watch over these children/this child
whom you have blessed with the grace of baptism.
When they/he/she have/has grown to maturity,
grant that they/he/she will confess your name in
willing faith,
be fervent in charity,
and persevere courageously in the hope of reaching
your kingdom,
where you live and reign for ever and ever.
R Amen.

The parents conclude the rite by signing themselves
with the sign of the cross and saying:

May the Lord Jesus, who loved children,
bless us and keep us in his love,
now and for ever.
R Amen.

A minister who is a priest or deacon concludes the rite
by saying:

May the Lord Jesus, who loved children,
bless you and keep you in his love,
now and for ever.
R Amen.

Short Formulary
As circumstances suggest, the following short blessing
formulary may be used:

May the Lord keep you
and make you grow in his love,
so that you may live worthy of the calling he has given
you,
now and for ever.
R Amen.

BLESSING OF CHILDREN
IN PREPARATION FOR BAPTISM
In the name of the Father and of the Son and of the
Holy Spirit.
R Amen.

One of those present reads a text of sacred scripture,
for example:

Brothers and sisters, listen to the words of the holy
gospel according to Matthew 19:13-15:

People brought little children to him, for him to lay his
hands on them and say a prayer. The disciples turned
them away, but Jesus said, 'Let the children alone, and

do not stop them coming to me; for it is to such as these that the kingdom of heaven belongs.' Then he laid his hands on them and went on his way.

The minister says the prayer of blessing:

All-powerful God and Father,
you are the source of all blessings, the protector of infants,
whose gift of children enriches and brightens a marriage.
Look with favour on this child
and, when he/she is reborn of water and the Holy Spirit,
bring him/her into your own spiritual family, the Church,
there to become a sharer in your kingdom
and with us to bless your name for ever.
Through Christ our Lord.
R Amen.

In silence the minister and the parents trace the sign of the cross on the child's forehead.

BLESSING OF CHILDREN
OF SEPARATED PEOPLE[5]

In the name of the Father and of the Son and of the Holy Spirit.
R Amen.

One of those present or the minister reads a text of sacred scripture, for example:

Let us listen to the words of the holy gospel according to Matthew 18:1-5:

At this time the disciples came to Jesus and said, 'Who is the greatest in the kingdom of Heaven?' So he called a little child to him and set the child in front of them. Then he said, 'I tell you solemnly, unless you change and become like little children you will never enter the kingdom of heaven. And so, the one who makes himself as little as this little child is the greatest in the kingdom of heaven. Anyone who welcomes a little child like this in my name welcomes me.'

Let us pray for N. (and N.).

May God bring comfort in times of loneliness. R God's love is without end.
May God bring peace in times of anguish. R
May God bring courage and security in times of fear. R
May God bring strength and light every day. R

---

[5] Adapted from the *Book of Blessings*, n. 1984ff

Bless your people, Lord,
who wait for the gift of your compassion.
Grant that what they desire by your inspiration
they may receive through your goodness.
Through Christ our Lord.

The minister concludes the rite by saying:

May God, who is blessed above all,
bless you in all things through Christ,
so that whatever happens in your lives
will work together for your good.
R Amen.

A priest or deacon continues:

And may almighty God bless you, the Father, and the
Son, ✠ and the Holy Spirit.
R Amen.

BLESSING OF A CHILD
WITH SPECIAL NEEDS[6]

In the name of the Father and of the Son and of the
Holy Spirit.
R Amen.

One of those present or the minister reads a text of
sacred scripture, for example:

Let us listen to the words of the holy gospel according
to Matthew 18:1-5:

---

[6] Adapted from the *Book of Blessings*, n. 1984ff

At this time the disciples came to Jesus and said, 'Who is the greatest in the kingdom of Heaven?' So he called a little child to him and set the child in front of them. Then he said, 'I tell you solemnly, unless you change and become like little children you will never enter the kingdom of heaven. And so, the one who makes himself as little as this little child is the greatest in the kingdom of heaven. Anyone who welcomes a little child like this in my name welcomes me.'

The minister introduces the intercessions:

God loves us and sustains us in his goodness. Let us ask his blessing on N. and on all of us gathered here.

One of those present, or the minister, continues:

Bless N. and surround him/her with constant love and care.
R Lord, hear our prayer.
Protect N. from danger and keep him/her safe. R
Give N. a future that is secure and happy. R
Bless N. with the knowledge of your love. R

The minister says the prayer of blessing:

Lord,
we, your people, pray for the gift of your holy blessing
to ward off every harm
and to bring to fulfilment every right desire.
Through Christ our Lord.
R Amen.

BLESSING OF AN INFANT
WITH SPECIAL NEEDS[7]

The pastoral care of parents whose infant has special needs validates the grief they may feel about the disappointments and challenges they and their child will face, while also helping them to accept their child and to be open to unexpected gifts from the Lord.

In the name of the Father and of the Son and of the Holy Spirit.
R Amen.

One of those present or the minister reads a text of sacred scripture, for example:

Brothers and sisters, listen to the words of the holy gospel according to John 9:1-3:

As he went along, he saw a man who had been blind from birth. His disciples asked him, 'Rabbi, who sinned, this man or his parents, for him to have been born blind?' 'Neither he nor his parents sinned,' Jesus answered, 'he was born blind so that the works of God might be displayed in him.'

The minister introduces the intercessions:

Let us renew our trust in God, praying for N. and for one another.

---

[7] Adapted from the *Book of Blessings*, n. 1984ff

Bless N., your child, that he/she may receive all the love and affection he/she will need to grow in love. R Lord, send us your blessing.

Strengthen and console N. and N. as they face the new challenges that face them in their lives as parents. R

Draw N.'s family closer together. May N. unlock within them deeper sources of love and compassion, that they may discover new and unexpected blessings. R

Help us all to become a more caring community, that we may be a source of strength and support to N.'s family. R

The minister says the prayer of blessing:

Bless your people, Lord,
who wait for the gift of your compassion.
Grant that what they desire by your inspiration
they may receive through your goodness.
Through Christ our Lord.

The minister concludes the rite by saying:

May God, who is blessed above all,
bless you in all things through Christ,
so that whatever happens in your lives
will work together for your good.
R Amen.

A priest or deacon continues:

And may almighty God bless you, the Father, and the Son, ✠ and the Holy Spirit.

R Amen.

BLESSING OF ORPHANS[8]

This order is for use by a priest or deacon.

In the name of the Father and of the Son and of the Holy Spirit.

R Amen.

One of those present, or the minister, reads a text of sacred scripture, for example, Matthew 18:5:

Anyone who welcomes a little child like this in my name welcomes me.

The minister blesses each child:

May the Lord Jesus, who loved children,
bless ✠ you, N., and keep you in his love,
now and for ever.

R Amen.

---

[8] Adapted from the *Book of Blessings*, n. 170ff

BLESSING OF AN ENGAGED COUPLE[9]

In the name of the Father and of the Son and of the Holy Spirit.

R Amen.

One of those present, or the minister, reads a text of sacred scripture, for example:

Brothers and sisters, listen to the words of the holy gospel according to John 15:9-12:

Jesus said to his disciples: 'As the Father has loved me, so I have loved you. Remain in my love. If you keep my commandments you will remain in my love, just as I have kept my Father's commandments and remain in his love. I have told you this so that my own joy may be in you and your joy might be complete. This is my commandment: love one another, as I have loved you.'

Before the blessing the engaged couple may express some sign of their pledge to each other, for example by exchanging rings or gifts. These may be blessed by use of the following formulary:

In due course may you honour the sacred pledge symbolised by these gifts which you now exchange.

R Amen.

---

[9] Adapted from the *Book of Blessings*, n. 199ff

The minister says the blessing prayer:

We praise you, Lord,
for your gentle plan draws together your children, N.
and N.,
in love for one another.
Strengthen their hearts,
so that they will keep faith with each other,
please you in all things, and so come to the happiness
of celebrating the sacrament
of their marriage.
Through Christ our Lord.
R Amen.

The minister concludes the rite by saying:

May the God of love and peace
abide in you, guide your steps,
and confirm your hearts in his love,
now and for ever.
R Amen.

BLESSING OF PARENTS BEFORE CHILDBIRTH[10]
It is appropriate that both parents receive God's blessing together as they wait in faith and hope for the birth of their child. A different prayer of blessing is given for use when only the mother is present.

In the name of the Father and of the Son and of the Holy Spirit.
R Amen.

One of those present, or the minister, reads a text of sacred scripture, for example:

Brothers and sisters, listen to the words of the holy gospel according to Luke 1:39-45:

Mary set out at that time and went as quickly as she could to a town in the hill country of Judah. She went into Zechariah's house and greeted Elizabeth. Now as soon as Elizabeth heard Mary's greeting, the child leapt in her womb and Elizabeth was filled with the holy Spirit. She gave a loud cry and said, 'Of all women you are the most blessed, and blessed is the fruit of your womb. Why should I be honoured with a visit from the mother of my Lord? For at the moment your greeting reached my ears, the child in my womb leapt for joy. Yes, blessed is she who believed that the promise made to her by the Lord would be fulfilled.'

The minister says the prayer of blessing:

Gracious Father,
your word, spoken in love, created the human family

---

[10] Adapted from the Book of Blessings, n. 215ff

and, in the fullness of time,
your Son, conceived in love, restored it to your
friendship.
Hear the prayers of N. and N.,
who await the birth of their child.
Calm their fears when they are anxious.
Watch over and support these parents
and bring their child into this world
safely and in good health,
so that as members of your family
they may praise you and glorify you
through your Son, our Lord Jesus Christ,
now and for ever.
R Amen.

As circumstances suggest, the following blessing may
be used when only the mother is present:

God has brought gladness and light to the world
through the Virgin Mary's delivery of her child.
May Christ fill your heart with his holy joy
and keep you and your baby safe from harm.

May God, who chose to make known and to send
the blessings of eternal salvation
through the motherhood of the Blessed Virgin,
bless us and keep us in his care, now and for ever.
R Amen.

Before the celebration concludes, there may be a
prayer to the Blessed Virgin, for example the Hail
Mary or the Hail Holy Queen or a Marian hymn.

BLESSING OF PARENTS OF A STILLBORN BABY OR AFTER A MISCARRIAGE[11]

In the name of the Father and of the Son and of the Holy Spirit.

R Amen.

In the following or similar words, the minister prepares those present for the blessing:

For those who trust in God,
in the pain of sorrow there is consolation,
in the face of despair there is hope,
in the midst of death there is life.
N. and N., as we mourn the death of your child
we place ourselves in the hands of God
and ask for strength, for healing, and for love.

One of those present, or the minister, reads a text of sacred scripture, for example:

Brothers and sisters, listen to the words of Lamentations 3:17-26:

My soul is shut out from peace;
I have forgotten happiness.
And now I say, 'My strength is gone,
That hope which came from the Lord.'

Brooding on my anguish and affliction
is gall and wormwood.
My spirit ponders it continually
and sinks within me.
This is what I shall tell my heart
and so recover hope:

---

[11] Adapted from the *Book of Blessings*, n. 282ff

the favours of the Lord are not all past,
his kindnesses are not exhausted;
every morning they are renewed;
great is his faithfulness.
'My portion is the Lord,' says my soul
'and so I will hope in him.'

The Lord is good to those who trust him,
to the soul that searches for him.
It is good to wait in silence
for the Lord to save.

The minister introduces the intercessions:

Let us pray to God who throughout the ages has heard
the cries of parents.
R Lord, hear our prayer.

Another person present, or the minister, continues:

For N. and N., who know the pain of grief, that they
may be comforted, we pray: R

For this family, that it may find new hope in the midst
of suffering, we pray: R

For these parents, that they may learn from the example
of Mary, who grieved by the cross of her Son, we pray: R

For all who have suffered the loss of a child, that
Christ may be their support, we pray: R

Some parents may wish an intercession such as the
following to be inserted:

For this little one, whom you formed in the womb, and
have known by name from the beginning of time,

whom we now name N., a name we shall treasure in our hearts for ever, we pray: R

After the intercessions the minister, in the following or similar words, invites all present to say the Lord's Prayer:

Let us pray to the God of consolation and hope, as Christ taught us:

All: Our Father ...

The minister says the prayer of blessing:

Compassionate God,
soothe the hearts of N. and N.,
and grant that through the prayers of Mary,
who grieved by the cross of her Son,
you may enlighten their faith,
give hope to their hearts
and peace to their lives.

Lord,
grant mercy to all the members of this family
and comfort them with the hope
that one day we will all live with you,
with your Son Jesus Christ and the Holy Spirit, for ever and ever.
R Amen.

As circumstances suggest, the minister may sprinkle the parents with holy water in silence.

BLESSING OF PARENTS[12]

In the name of the Father and of the Son and of the Holy Spirit.

R Amen.

One of those present, or the minister, reads a text of sacred scripture, for example:

Brothers and sisters, listen to the words of the holy gospel according to Luke 2:41-52:

Every year his parents used to go to Jerusalem for the feast of the Passover. When he was twelve years old, they went up for the feast as usual. When they were on their way home after the feast, the boy Jesus stayed behind in Jerusalem without his parents knowing it. They assumed he was with the caravan, and it was only after a day's journey that they went to look for him among their relations and acquaintances. When they failed to find him they went back to Jerusalem looking for him everywhere.

Three days later, they found him in the Temple, sitting among the doctors, listening to them, and asking them questions; and all those who heard him were astounded at his intelligence and his replies. They were overcome when they saw him, and his mother said to him, 'My child, why have you done this to us? See how worried your father and I have been, looking for you.' 'Why were you looking for me?' he replied 'Did you not know that I must be busy with my Father's affairs?' But they did not understand what he meant.

---

[12] Adapted from the *Book of Blessings*, n. 1984ff

He then went down with them and came to Nazareth and lived under their authority. His mother stored up all these things in her heart. And Jesus increased in wisdom, in stature, and in favour with God and men.

The minister says:

Let us pray to the Lord, who watches over us with fatherly care.
R Lord, send us your blessing.

One of those present, or the minister, continues:

Support us as we care for one another and for our children. R

Give us strength and patience to cope with the many ups and downs of family life. R

Give us the grace to be deeply thankful for its many laughs, joys and blessings. R

May our children come to know of your love through our own loving care for them. R

May our home be a place where love dwells, like that of Jesus, Mary and Joseph in Nazareth. R

When we fail each other, may we be swift to seek and to give forgiveness. R

Protect our family, that it may flourish in your light and in your love. R

The minister says the prayer of blessing:

Lord God,
from the abundance of your mercy
enrich your servants and safeguard them.
Strengthened by your blessing,
may they always be thankful to you
and bless you with unending joy.

Through Christ our Lord.
R Amen.

BLESSING OF PARENTS OF A CHILD WITH SPECIAL NEEDS[13]

In the name of the Father and of the Son and of the Holy Spirit.

R Amen.

One of those present, or the minister, reads a text of sacred scripture, for example:

Brothers and sisters, listen to the words of the holy gospel according to Matthew 18:1-4:

At this time the disciples came to Jesus and said, 'Who is the greatest in the kingdom of Heaven?' So he called a little child to him and set the child in front of them. Then he said, 'I tell you solemnly, unless you change and become like little children you will never enter the kingdom of heaven. And so, the one who makes himself as little as this little child is the greatest in the kingdom of heaven. Anyone who welcomes a little child like this in my name welcomes me.'

The minister introduces the intercessions:

Let us pray to the Lord,
asking for strength and support.
R Lord, send us your blessing.

---

[13] Adapted from the *Book of Blessings*, n. 1984ff

May life with N. lead us in the ways of faith, hope, confidence and love. R

May the burdens of parenthood not blind us to the blessings you have prepared for us. R

May your Holy Spirit of Wisdom guide our every action. R

May the prayers of Mary, who accepted the sword of suffering in her own life, help us to accept in trust the burdens of each day. R

Lord,
let the effect of your blessing
remain with your faithful people,
to give them new life and strength of spirit,
so that the power of your love
will enable them to accomplish what is right and good.
Through Christ our Lord.
R Amen.

BLESSING OF PARENTS AND AN ADOPTED CHILD[14]

In the name of the Father and of the Son and of the Holy Spirit.

R Amen.

A reader, another person present or the minister reads a text of sacred scripture, for example:

Brothers and sisters, listen to the words of the holy gospel according to Mark 10:13-16:

People were bringing little children to him, for him to touch them. The disciples turned them away, but when Jesus saw this he was indignant and said to them, 'Let the little children come to me; do not stop them; for it is to such as these that the kingdom of God belongs. I tell you solemnly, anyone who does not welcome the kingdom of God like a little child will never enter it.' Then he put his arms round them, laid his hands on them and gave them his blessing.

The minister asks the parents:

You have received N. into your family; will you (continue to) love and care for him/her?

Parents:

We will.

---

[14] Adapted from the *Book of Blessings*, n. 302ff

If appropriate, the minister asks the child:

You have accepted N. and N. as your parents; will you love and respect them?

The child replies:

I will.

The minister says:

As God has made us all his children by grace and adoption, may this family always abide in his love.

The minister introduces the intercessions:

God is the author of all life and calls us into his loving family; with thankful hearts we pray: Lord, hear us.
R Lord, graciously hear us.

The minister or another person present announces the intentions:

Let us pray for the Church throughout the world, that it may nurture, guide, protect and love all who are joined to it in baptism. Lord, hear us.

Let us pray for N. and N. and their new son/daughter, N., that God may bind them together in love as a family in Christ. Lord, hear us.

Let us pray for the brother(s) and sister(s) of N., that they may grow in friendship and love. Lord, hear us.

Let us pray for married couples who desire the gift of a child, that God may hear their prayers. Lord, hear us.

The minister invites all present to pray the Lord's prayer:

All: Our Father...

The minister says the prayer of blessing:

Loving God,
your Son has taught us
that whoever welcomes a child in his name, welcomes him.
We give you thanks for N.,
whom N. and N. have welcomed into their family.
Bless this family.
Confirm a lively sense of your presence with them
and grant to these parents patience and wisdom,
that their lives may show forth the love of Christ
as they bring N. up to love all that is good.
Through Christ our Lord.
R Amen.

As circumstances suggest, the minister may sprinkle the family with holy water.

A minister who is a priest or deacon concludes the rite by saying:

May almighty God, who has called us into the family of Christ, fill you with grace and peace, now and for ever.
R Amen.

Then he blesses all present:

And may almighty God bless you all, the Father, and
the Son, ✠ and the Holy Spirit.
R Amen.

A lay minister concludes the rite by signing himself or
herself with the sign of the cross and saying:

May almighty God, who has called us into the family
of Christ, fill us with grace and peace, now and
forever.
R Amen.

In addition to suggestions given on page 17, this
celebration may also include the Canticle of Mary or
another hymn of praise before the intercessions.

BLESSING OF A CHILDLESS COUPLE[15]

In the name of the Father and of the Son and of the
Holy Spirit.

R Amen.

A reader, another person present or the minister reads
a text of sacred scripture, for example:

Brothers and sisters, listen to the words of
Ecclesiasticus 2:3-12:

Cling to him and do not leave him,
    so that you may be honoured at the end of your days.
Whatever happens to you, accept it,
    and in the uncertainties of your humble state,
      be patient,
since gold is tested in the fire,
    and chosen men in the furnace of humiliation.
Trust him and he will uphold you,
    follow a straight path and hope in him.
You who fear the Lord, wait for his mercy;
    do not turn aside in case you fall.
You who fear the Lord, trust him,
    and you will not be baulked of your reward.
You who fear the Lord hope for good things,
    for everlasting happiness and mercy.
Look at the generations of old and see:
    who ever trusted in the Lord and was put to shame?
Or who ever feared him steadfastly and was left
    forsaken?
Or who ever called out to him, and was ignored?

---

[15] Adapted from the *Book of Blessings*, n. 1984ff

The minister says:

God loves his creation and his goodness sustains the universe. Let us pray now that he will bestow his blessing upon us and that he will renew and support us with his strength.

R Lord, send us your blessing.

God of mercy and compassion, fill us with the spirit of your own holiness. R

You watch over us with fatherly care; hear the prayers of those who trust in you. R

Bless N. and N., whose love has grown throughout their married life, and crown their love with the gift of new life. R

Help them to accept your will in their lives and let their love bring joy to the world. R

May the peace and joy of Nazareth be always in their home, as they place all their trust in you. R

The prayer of blessing follows:

Lord,
may the blessing they long for
be the strength of your faithful people,
so that they will never be in conflict with your will.
May your blessing always prompt them
to give thanks for your favours.
Through Christ our Lord.

The minister concludes the rite by saying:

May God, who is blessed above all,
bless you in all things through Christ,
so that whatever happens in your lives
will work together for your good.
R Amen.

A priest or deacon continues:

And may almighty God bless you, the Father, and the
Son, ✠ and the Holy Spirit.
R Amen.

BLESSING OF A PARTNER FOLLOWING SEPARATION/
DIVORCE[16]

In the name of the Father and of the Son and of the
Holy Spirit.
R Amen.

A reader, another person present or the minister reads
a text of sacred scripture, for example:

Brothers and sisters, listen to the book of the prophet
Isaiah 43:1-2, 4a:

Do not be afraid, for I have redeemed you;
I have called you by your name, you are mine.
Should you pass through the sea, I will be with you;
or through rivers, they will not swallow you up.
Should you walk through fire, you will not be
scorched,
and the flames will not burn you.
For I am the Lord, your God,
the Holy One of Israel, your saviour …
Because you are precious in my eyes,
Because you are honoured and I love you.

The minister says:

Let us pray to God, whose tender mercy is without end.

Everlasting God, whose healing love reaches into the
depths of our hearts,
look with kindness on N..
R Lord, send us your blessing.

---

[16] Adapted from the *Book of Blessings*, n. 1984ff

Give him/her comfort when he/she is lonely. R

Give him/her your consolation when he/she is weighed down with sorrow. R

Give him/her courage when he/she is afraid. R

May your Holy Spirit lead N. forward on a journey of healing. R

May he/she in time rediscover peace and joy, flowing from your hand. R

The prayer of blessing follows:

Bless your people, Lord,
who wait for the gift of your compassion.
Grant that what they desire by your inspiration
they may receive through your goodness.
Through Christ our Lord.

The minister concludes the rite by saying:

May God, who is blessed above all,
bless you in all things through Christ,
so that whatever happens in your lives
will work together for your good.
R Amen.

A priest or deacon continues:

And may almighty God bless you, the Father, and the Son, ✠ and the Holy Spirit.
R Amen.

BLESSING ON THE OCCASION
OF A BIRTHDAY[17]

In the name of the Father and of the Son and of the
Holy Spirit.
R Amen.

One of those present, or the minister, reads a text of
sacred scripture, for example:

Brothers and sisters, listen to the prophet Hosea 11:3-4:

I myself taught Ephraim to walk,
I took them in my arms;
yet they have not understood that I was the one
looking after them.
I lead them with reins of kindness,
with leading-strings of love.
I was like someone who lifts an infant close against his
cheek;
stooping down to him I gave him his food.

The minister says the prayer of blessing:

A. For adults
God of all creation,
we offer you grateful praise for the gift of life.
Hear the prayers of N., your servant,
who recalls today the day of his/her birth
and rejoices in your gifts of life and love, family and
friends.

---

[17] Adapted from the *Book of Blessings*, n. 323ff

Bless him/her with your presence
and surround him/her with your love
that he/she may enjoy many happy years,
all of them pleasing to you.
Through Christ our Lord.
R Amen.

B. For children

Loving God,
you created all the people of the world
and you know each of us by name.
We thank you for N., who today celebrates his/her birthday.
Bless him/her with your love and friendship
that he/she may grow in wisdom, knowledge, and grace.
May he/she love his/her family always
and be faithful to his/her friends.
Through Christ our Lord.
R Amen.

BLESSING OF AN ELDERLY PERSON CONFINED TO HOME[18]

The prayer of blessing given below may also be used when the person receives Holy Communion outside Mass. A longer celebration might be suitable when a number of people are being blessed together, for example, in a nursing home. See page 17 for suggestions.

In the name of the Father and of the Son and of the Holy Spirit.
R Amen.

One of those present, or the minister, reads a text of sacred scripture, for example:

Brothers and sisters, listen to the words of the letter of St Paul to the Romans 8:35, 37-39:

Nothing therefore can come between us and the love of Christ, even if we are troubled or worried, or being persecuted, or lacking food or clothes, or being threatened or even attacked ... These are the trials through which we triumph, by the power of him who loved us. For I am certain of this: neither death nor life, no angel, no prince, nothing that exists, nothing still to come, not any power, or height or depth, nor any created thing, can ever come between us and the love of God made visible in Jesus Christ our Lord.

---

[18] Adapted from the *Book of Blessings*, n. 372ff

A minister who is a priest or deacon may extend his hands over the elderly person or trace the sign of the cross on the elderly person's forehead, as he says the prayer of blessing; a lay minister says the prayer with hands joined:

Lord God almighty,
bless your servant, N.,
to whom you have given a long life.
Let him/her be aware of your nearness,
so that when he/she worries about past failings,
he/she will rejoice in your mercy
and, when he/she thinks of the future,
he/she will faithfully rely on you as his/her hope.
Through Christ our Lord.
R Amen.

BLESSINGS OF THE SICK

Pastoral ministers are advised to look to the *Pastoral Care of the Sick* for a fuller compendium of texts and rites. In particular, the Sacrament of Anointing of the Sick is appropriately used at the onset of serious illness and moments of progressive illness.

BLESSING OF ADULTS WHO ARE SICK[19]
In the name of the Father and of the Son and of the Holy Spirit.
R Amen.

One of those present, or the minister, reads a text of sacred scripture, for example:

Brothers and sisters, listen to the words of the holy gospel according to Matthew 11:28-30:

Come to me, all you who labour and are overburdened, and I will give you rest. Shoulder my yoke and learn from me, for I am gentle and humble in heart, *and you will find rest for souls*. Yes, my yoke is easy and my burden light.

Or

2 Cor 1:3-7 *The God of all consolation*
Mk 6:53-56 *They laid the sick in the marketplace*

---

[19] Adapted from the *Book of Blessings*, n. 380ff

The minister may lead the following short litany or, instead, intercessions composed specially for the occasion.

You bore our weakness and carried our sorrows: Lord, have mercy. R Lord, have mercy.

You felt compassion for the crowd, and went about doing good and healing the sick: Christ, have mercy. R Christ, have mercy.

You commanded your apostles to lay their hands on the sick in your name: Lord, have mercy. R Lord, have mercy.

A minister who is a priest or deacon may, as circumstances suggest, lay his hands on the head of each sick person, and then say the prayer of blessing:

Lord, our God,
you sent your Son into the world
to bear our infirmities
and to endure our sufferings.
For N. and N., your servants who are sick,
we ask that your blessing will give them strength
to overcome their weakness
through the power of patience and the comfort of hope
and that with your aid they will soon be restored to health.
Through Christ our Lord.
R Amen.

Or, without the laying on of hands:

Lord Jesus,
who went about doing good and healing all,
we ask you to bless your friends who are sick.

Give them strength in body, courage in spirit, and
patience with pain.
Let them recover their health,
so that, restored to the Christian community,
they may joyfully praise your name,
for you live and reign for ever and ever.
R Amen.

A lay person traces the sign of the cross on the
forehead of each sick person and says the following
prayer of blessing:

Lord, our God,
who watch over your creatures with unfailing care,
keep us in the safe embrace of your love.
With your strong right hand raise up your servants N.
and N.
and give them the strength of your own power.
Minister to them and heal their illnesses,
so that they may have from you the help they long for.
Through Christ our Lord.

Or, for one sick person:

Lord and Father, almighty and eternal God,
by your blessing you give us strength and support in
our frailty:
turn with kindness toward this your servant N..

Free him/her from all illness and restore him/her to health,
so that in the sure knowledge of your goodness
he/she will gratefully bless your holy name.
Through Christ our Lord.
R Amen.

After the prayer of blessing, the minister may invite all present to pray for the protection of the Blessed Virgin, by praying, for example, the Hail Mary, the Hail, Holy Queen or by singing a suitable Marian hymn.

A minister who is a priest or deacon concludes the rite by facing the sick and saying:

May God the Father bless you. R Amen.

May God the Son comfort you. R Amen.

May God the Holy Spirit enlighten you. R Amen.

Then he blesses all present:

And may almighty God bless you all, the Father, and the Son, ✠ and the Holy Spirit.
R Amen.

A lay minister invokes the Lord's blessing on the sick and all present by signing himself or herself with the sign of the cross and saying:

May the Lord Jesus Christ,
who went about doing good and healing the sick,
grant that we may have good health
and be enriched by his blessings.
R Amen.

BLESSING OF CHILDREN WHO ARE SICK[20]
If the child does not already know the minister, it is helpful if the minister seeks first to establish a friendly and easy rapport with the child. Thus it may be a good idea to have some informal interaction with the child before beginning the rite of blessing.

Some adaptation of the texts given here may be needed, according to circumstances.

In the name of the Father and of the Son and of the Holy Spirit.
R Amen.

One of those present, or the minister, reads a text of sacred scripture, for example:

Brothers and sisters, listen to the words of the holy gospel according to Mark 10:13-16:

People where bringing little children to him, for him to touch them. The disciples turned them away, but when Jesus saw this he was indignant and said to them, 'Let the little children come to me; do not stop them; for it is to such as these that the kingdom of God belongs. I tell you solemnly, anyone who does not welcome the kingdom of God like a little child will never enter it.' Then he put his arms around them, laid his hands on them and gave them his blessing.

---

[20] Adapted from the *Book of Blessings*, n. 399ff

The minister may introduce some intercessions, as follows:

Let us pray to the Lord for N..

Another person present, or the minister, continues:

Show N. your loving kindness.
R Lord, hear our prayer.

Strengthen N. and give him/her comfort. R

Bless N.'s parents who love him/her. R

Give your blessing to all sick children and to those who care for them. R

A minister who is a priest or deacon may, as circumstances suggest, lay his hands on the head of the sick child, and then say the prayer of blessing:

Lord, our God,
your Son Jesus Christ welcomed little children and blessed them.
Stretch out your right hand over this little child N. who is sick.
Grant that, made well again,
he/she may return to his/her parents
and to the community of your holy Church
and give you thanks and praise.
Through Christ our Lord.
R Amen.

A lay minister, and particularly a mother or father when blessing a sick child, traces the sign of the cross on the child's forehead and then says the following prayer of blessing:

Father of mercy and God of all consolation,
you show tender care for all your creatures
and give health of soul and body.
Raise up this child (or the son/daughter you have given us) from his/her sickness.
Then, growing in wisdom and grace in your sight and in ours,
he/she will serve you all the days of his/her life in uprightness and holiness
and offer the thanksgiving due to your mercy.
Through Christ our Lord.
R Amen.

SHORT FORMULARY FOR THE BLESSING OF THE SICK[21]

As circumstances suggest, a priest or deacon may use the following short blessing formulary:

May he who alone is Lord and Redeemer bless you, N.
May he give health to your body
and holiness to your soul.
May he bring you safely to eternal life.
R Amen.

---

[21] From the *Book of Blessings*, n. 406

BLESSING OF A PERSON SUFFERING FROM MENTAL ILLNESS[22]

In the name of the Father and of the Son and of the Holy Spirit.

R Amen.

One of those present, or the minister, reads a text of sacred scripture, for example 2 Corinthians 1:3-4:

Blessed be the God and Father of our Lord Jesus Christ, a gentle father and the God of all consolation, who comforts us in our all our sorrows, so that we can offer others, in their sorrows, the consolation that we have received from God ourselves.

As circumstances suggest, a minister who is a priest or deacon may lay hands on the sick person while saying the prayer of blessing; a lay minister may trace the sign of the cross on the sick person's head while saying the following prayer:

Lord and Father, almighty and eternal God,
by your blessing you give us strength and support in our frailty:
turn with kindness toward this your servant N..
Free him/her from all illness and restore him/her to health,
so that in the sure knowledge of your goodness
he/she will gratefully bless your holy name.
Through Christ our Lord.

R Amen.

---

[22] From the *Book of Blessings*, n. 403ff

BLESSING OF A PERSON SUFFERING FROM ADDICTION[23]

In the name of the Father and of the Son and of the Holy Spirit.

R Amen.

One of those present, or the minister, reads a text of sacred scripture, for example:

Brothers and sisters, listen to the words of the second letter of Paul to the Corinthians 4:6-10:

It is the same God that said 'Let there be light shining out of darkness', who has shone in minds to radiate the light of the knowledge of God's glory, the glory on the face of Christ.

We are the earthenware jars that hold this treasure, to make it clear that such an overwhelming power comes from God and not from us. We are in difficulties on all sides, but never cornered; we see no answer to our problems, but never despair; we have been persecuted, but never deserted; knocked down but never killed.

The minister says the prayer of blessing:

God of mercy,
we bless you in the name of your Son, Jesus Christ,
who ministered to all who came to him.
Give your strength to N., your servant,
enfold him/her in your love
and restore him/her to the freedom of God's children.

---

[23] Adapted from the *Book of Blessings*, n. 426ff

Lord, look with compassion on all those
who have lost their health and freedom.
Restore to them the assurance of your unfailing mercy,
strengthen them in the work of recovery,
and help them to resist all temptation.

To those who care for them,
grant patient understanding and a love that perseveres.
Through Christ our Lord.
R Amen.

PRAYER FOR A PERSON SUFFERING FROM DEPRESSION[24]

In the name of the Father and of the Son and of the Holy Spirit.

R Amen.

One of those present, or the minister, reads a text of sacred scripture, for example:

Let us listen to the words of the holy gospel according to Matthew 11:28-30:

Come to me, all you who labour and are overburdened, and I will give you rest. Shoulder my yoke and learn from me, for I am gentle and humble in heart, *and you will find rest for souls*. Yes, my yoke is easy and my burden light.

The Lord is my light and my help;
whom shall I fear?
The Lord is the stronghold of my life;
before whom shall I shrink? R The Lord is my light and my help.

For there he keeps me safe in his tent
in the day of evil.
He hides me in the shelter of his tent,
on a rock he sets me safe. R

---

[24] Adapted from *Pastoral Care of the Sick*, no. 57ff

The minister may then give a brief explanation of the reading, applying it to the needs of the person.
The minister introduces the Lord's Prayer.

All say: **Our Father …**

The minister says a concluding prayer:

All-powerful and ever-living God,
we find security in your forgiveness.
Give us serenity and peace of mind;
may we rejoice in your gifts of kindness
and use them always for your glory and our good.
Through Christ our Lord.
R **Amen.**

The minister may give a blessing:

All praise and glory is yours, Lord our God,
for you have called us to serve you in love.
Bless N. so that he/she may bear this illness
in union with your Son's obedient suffering.
Restore him/her to health, and lead him/her to glory.
Through Christ our Lord.
R **Amen.**

If the minister is a priest or deacon, he immediately concludes:

May the blessing of almighty God, the Father, and the Son, ✠ and the Holy Spirit, come upon you and remain with you for ever.

The priest may lay hands upon the person's head.

R Amen.

A minister who is not a priest or deacon invokes God's blessing and makes the sign of the cross on himself or herself, while saying:

May the Lord bless us,
protect us from all evil,
and bring us to everlasting life.
R Amen.

The minister may then trace the sign of the cross on the person's forehead.

BLESSING OF A PERSON DISABLED THROUGH AN ACCIDENT[25]

In the name of the Father and of the Son and of the Holy Spirit.
R Amen.

One of those present, or the minister, reads a text of sacred scripture, for example:

Let us listen to the words of St Paul's letter to the Romans 8:35-37:

Nothing therefore can come between us and the love of Christ, even if we are troubled or worried, or being persecuted, or lacking food or clothes, or being threatened or even attacked. As scripture promised: *For your sake we are being massacred daily, and reckoned as sheep for the slaughter.* These are the trials through which we triumph, by the power of him who loved us.

The minister introduces the intercessions:

Let us pray that God will bestow his blessing upon us, renewing and supporting us with his strength.

Another person present, or the minister, continues:

Bless N. in your love, that he/she may experience the help and concern of others.
R Lord, send us your blessing.

---

[25] Adapted from the *Book of Blessings*, n. 1984ff

Unite him/her closely to the humanity of Jesus Christ
your Son, who gave his life for us. R

Renew within him/her the power and vitality of the
Holy Spirit. R

Helps us all to experience your power at work in our
weakness. R

The minister says the prayer of blessing:

Lord,
let the effect of your blessing
remain with your faithful people
to give them new life and strength of spirit,
so that the power of your love
will enable them to accomplish what is right and good.
Through Christ our Lord.

The minister concludes the rite by saying:

May God, who is blessed above all,
bless you in all things through Christ,
so that whatever happens in your lives
will work together for your good.
R Amen.

A priest or deacon continues:

And may almighty God bless you, the Father, and the
Son, ✠ and the Holy Spirit.
R Amen.

BLESSING OF THOSE WHO HAVE BEEN BEREAVED[26]

In the name of the Father and of the Son and of the Holy Spirit.
R Amen.

In the following or similar words, the minister prepares those present for the blessing:

For those who trust in God, in the pain of sorrow there is consolation, in the face of despair there is hope, in the midst of death there is life. As we mourn the loss of N. we place ourselves in the hands of God and ask for strength, for healing, and for love.

One of those present, or the minister, reads a text of sacred scripture, for example:

Brothers and sisters, listen to the words of the book of Lamentations 3:17-26:

My soul is shut out from peace,
I have forgotten happiness.
And now I say, 'My strength is gone,
that hope which came from the Lord.'
Brooding on my anguish and affliction
is gall and wormwood.
My spirit ponders it continually
and sinks within me.

---

[26] Adapted from the *Book of Blessings*, n. 279ff

This is what I shall tell my heart,
and so recover hope:
The favours of the Lord are not all past,
his kindnesses are not exhausted;
every morning they are renewed;
great is his faithfulness.
'My portion is the Lord,' says my soul;
'and so I will hope in him.'
The Lord is good to those who trust him,
to the soul that searches for him;
It is good to wait in silence
for the Lord to save.

Some intercessions may follow.

The following intercessions may be suitable for the
blessing of a widow or a widower:

Let us pray to God, whose love is stronger than death.
R Lord, give us your blessing.

Look with compassion on N., whose marriage
reflected the love of Christ and Church. R

Strengthen N. who is now without his/her companion
in marriage. R

Keep alive in him/her the hope of one day being
reunited with the one whom he/she loves. R

The minister then says the prayer of blessing:

Compassionate God,
soothe the hearts of N. and N.,
and grant that through the prayers of Mary,
who grieved by the cross of her Son,
you may enlighten their faith,
give hope to their hearts,
and peace to their lives.

Lord,
grant mercy to all the members of this family (or this community)
and comfort them with the hope
that one day we will all live with you,
with your Son Jesus Christ, and the Holy Spirit,
for ever and ever.
R Amen.

As circumstances suggest, the minister may sprinkle those present with holy water.

See also prayers for the dead, pages 233–36.

BLESSING OF A SURVIVOR OF CRIME, ABUSE OR OPPRESSION[27]

In the name of the Father and of the Son and of the Holy Spirit.
R Amen.

One of those present, or the minister, reads a text of sacred scripture, for example:

Brothers and sisters, listen to the words of the book of Lamentations 3:17-26:

My soul is shut out from peace,
I have forgotten happiness.
And now I say, 'My strength is gone,
that hope which came from the Lord.'
Brooding on my anguish and affliction
is gall and wormwood.
My spirit ponders it continually
and sinks within me.
This is what I shall tell my heart,
and so recover hope:
The favours of the Lord are not all past,
his kindnesses are not exhausted;
every morning they are renewed;
great is his faithfulness.
'My portion is the Lord,' says my soul;
'and so I will hope in him.'
The Lord is good to those who trust him,
to the soul that searches for him;
It is good to wait in silence.

---

[27] Adapted from the *Book of Blessings*, n. 430ff

The minister then says the prayer of blessing:

Lord God,
your own Son was delivered into the hands of the wicked,
yet he prayed for his persecutors
and overcame hatred with the blood of his cross.
Relieve the suffering of N.;
grant him/her peace of mind
and a renewed faith in your protection and care.

Protect us all from the violence of others,
keep us safe from the weapons of hate,
and restore to us tranquility and peace.

Through Christ our Lord.
R Amen.

BLESSING OF MISSIONARIES SENT TO PROCLAIM THE GOSPEL[28]

Blessing Within Mass

Choice of Mass texts:

On solemnities and on the Sundays of Advent, Lent and the Easter season the Mass is the Mass of the day.

On the Sundays of the Christmas season and in Ordinary Time, on feasts, and on memorials the Mass may be either the Mass of the day or the Mass 'For the Spread of the Gospel'.

If the rubrics permit, instead of the readings assigned for the day, those given in the Lectionary for Mass from Masses for Various Needs and Occasions 'For the Spread of the Gospel' may be used.

Order of Blessing:

The liturgy of the word is carried out in the usual manner, with the following changes:

It is appropriate that, before the proclamation of the gospel reading, the missionaries be introduced by name to the congregation by a deacon or other assisting minister. When their names are called, the missionaries respond by word, for example, by saying 'Present', or by gesture, for example, by standing.

---

[28] Adapted from the *Book of Blessings*, n. 451ff

Before the gospel is proclaimed the celebrant addresses the following or similar words to the assisting minister who will proclaim the gospel and to all the missionaries (if there is a gospel procession with incense this is done after incense is put in the thurible):

By your words and your lives proclaim to all peoples the gospel that is proclaimed in this house of God, so that the mystery of Christ and the Church may be revealed to all.

The assisting minister and missionaries reply:

Amen.

After the homily all stand. The missionaries take places near the celebrant, but in such a way as not to obstruct the people's view of the rite. With hands outstretched over the missionaries as a group, the celebrant says the prayer of blessing:

We bless you, O God, and we praise your name.
In your merciful providence you sent your Son into the world
to free us from the bondage of sin by his own blood
and to enrich us with the gifts of the Holy Spirit.

Before he returned, triumphant over death, to you, Father,
he sent his apostles, the bearers of his love and power,
to proclaim the gospel of life to all peoples
and in the waters of baptism to cleanse those who believe.

Lord, look kindly on your servants:
we send them forth as messengers of salvation and peace,
marked with the sign of the cross.

Guide their steps with your mighty arm
and with the power of your grace strengthen them in spirit,
so that they will not falter through weariness.

Make their words the echo of Christ's voice,
so that those who hear them
may be drawn to obey the gospel.

Fill the hearts of your missionaries with the Holy Spirit,
so that, becoming all things to all people,
they may lead many to you, the Father of all,
to sing your praises in your holy Church.

Through Christ our Lord.
R Amen.

The celebrant may bless crosses and present them to the missionaries, as follows:

The celebrant says the prayer of blessing:

Father of holiness,
you willed the cross of your Son
to be the source of all blessings,
the fount of all grace.
Bless these crosses
and grant that those who will preach the crucified Christ to others
may themselves strive to be transformed into his image.

We ask this in the name of Jesus the Lord.
R Amen.

Then, one by one, the missionaries go to the celebrant, who gives each one a cross as he says:

Receive this sign of Christ's love and of our faith.
Preach Christ crucified,
who is the power and wisdom of God.

The missionary replies:

Amen.

Then the missionary takes the cross, kisses it and returns to his or her place.

Alternatively, the minister may say the formulary of presentation just once, with the missionaries replying Amen together, before each goes to receive a cross.

The presentation of crosses may be accompanied by the singing of a suitable song.

Blessing Outside Mass
The blessing may take place within a celebration of the Word of God, using readings and prayers as given above. In this case, intercessions are made after the homily and the prayer of blessing replaces the usual conclusion to the intercessions. It is suitable for the celebration to conclude with a solemn blessing.

BLESSING OF STUDENTS AND TEACHERS[29]

While this order of blessing is for both students and teachers, the prayer of blessing should be adapted when either students or teachers alone are blessed.

Blessing Within Mass
If the blessing is to be given during Mass, the blessing prayer Lord God, given on the next page, is said as a conclusion to the general intercessions.

Blessing Outside Mass
In the name of the Father and of the Son and of the Holy Spirit.
R Amen.

One of those present, or the minister, reads a text of sacred scripture, for example:

Brothers and sisters, listen to the words of the book of Ecclesiasticus 6:32:

If you wish, my son, you can aquire instruction;
if you give your mind to it, subtlety will be yours.
If you love listening, you will learn,
if you lend an ear, wisdom will be yours.

---

[29] Adapted from the *Book of Blessings*, n. 522ff

Alternatively, it may be preferable to use a scripture text that has been studied in class, or that relates to topics covered in class. As circumstances suggest, the minister may briefly explain the scripture text in the context of this celebration.

Some intercessions may follow. As well as referring to concerns proper to the class or school, the intercessions may touch on some of the following:

- development of talents
- development of self-control, integrity and honesty
- knowledge of Jesus Christ
- exploration of the reality of our world
- discernment of good and evil
- education of those who are deprived in any way
- blessing of teachers

The minister invites all present to sing or say the Lord's Prayer:

All: Our Father ...

The minister says the prayer of blessing:

Lord God,
your Spirit of wisdom fills the earth
and teaches us your ways.

Look upon these students.
Let them enjoy their learning
and take delight in new discoveries.
Help them to persevere in their studies
and give them the desire to learn all things well.

Look upon these teachers.
Let them strive to share their knowledge with gentle patience
and endeavour always to bring the truth to eager minds.

Grant that students and teachers alike may follow Jesus Christ,
the way, the truth, and the life.
R Amen.

See also the prayer for teachers of the young, given on page 245.

BLESSINGS OF THOSE GATHERED AT A MEETING

PRAYER FOR MEETINGS[30]

Come, Holy Spirit, fill the hearts of your faithful.
R   And kindle in them the fire of your love.
Send forth your Spirit and they shall be created.
R   And you will renew the face of the earth.

Let us pray.

After a brief pause for silent prayer, the leader continues:

Lord,
by the light of the Holy Spirit
you have taught the hearts of your faithful.
In the same Spirit
help us to relish what is right
and always rejoice in your consolation.
Through Christ our Lord.
R Amen.

---

[30] From the *Book of Blessings*, n. 552

BLESSING OF ECUMENICAL GROUPS[31]
In the name of the Father and of the Son and of the Holy Spirit.
R Amen.

One of those present, or the minister, reads a text of sacred scripture, for example:

Brothers and sisters, listen to the words of the apostle Paul to the Ephesians 4:1-6:

I, the prisoner in the Lord, implore you therefore to lead a life worthy of your vocation. Bear with one another charitably, in complete selflessness, gentleness and patience. Do all you can to preserve the unity of the Spirit by the peace that binds you together. There is one Body, one Spirit, just as you were all called into one and the same hope when you were called. There is one Lord, one faith, one baptism and one God who is Father of all, over all, through all and within all.

The minister says the prayer of blessing:

Lord God,
whose blessings reach to the ends of the earth,
you show us your love in the life, death and resurrection of Jesus,
whom we call Saviour and Lord.

---

[31] Adapted from the *Book of Blessings*, n. 556ff

Confirm us in our common faith
that we may walk together with you and one another.
Send your blessing upon your Church
that what we have begun in the Spirit
may be brought to completion by your power.

To you be glory and honour, now and for ever.
R Amen.

PRAYERS FOR INTERFAITH GATHERINGS[32]
Prayer of Invocation
In you, Lord our God,
all things have their beginning, continuation, and end.
Grace us with your saving presence,
aid us with your constant help
and let us glorify you, now and for ever
R Amen.

Blessing
May the Lord bless you and keep you.
May his face shine upon you and be gracious to you.
May he look upon you with kindness and give you his peace.
R Amen.

---

[32] From the *Book of Blessings*, n. 572-573

PRAYER BEFORE MAKING AN IMPORTANT DECISION[33]

A reading from the Book of Tobit 4:18-19:

Ask advice of every wise person; never scorn any profitable advice. Bless the Lord God in everything; beg him to guide your ways and bring your paths and purposes to their end.

Lord,
may everything we do
begin with your inspiration
and continue with your help,
so that all our prayers and works
may begin in you
and by you be happily ended.
Through Christ our Lord.
R Amen.

---

[33] From the *Book of Blessings*, n. 552

BLESSING OF GROUPS DEDICATED IN A SPECIAL WAY TO THE SERVICE OF THOSE IN NEED[34]

This order may be used by a priest or deacon.

In the name of the Father and of the Son and of the Holy Spirit.
R Amen.

One of those present, or the minister, reads a text of sacred scripture, for example:

Brothers and sisters, listen to the words of the holy gospel according to Matthew 25:31-40:

Jesus said to his disciples:

When the Son of Man comes in his glory, escorted by all the angels, then he will take his seat on his throne of glory. All the nations will be assembled before him and he will separate men one from another as the shepherd separates sheep from goats. He will place the sheep on his right hand and the goats on his left. Then the King will say to those on his right hand, 'Come, you whom my Father has blessed, take for your heritage the kingdom prepared for you since the foundation of the world. For I was hungry and you gave me food; I was thirsty and you gave me drink; I was a stranger and you made me welcome, naked and you clothed me, sick and visited me, in prison and came to see me.' Then the virtuous will say to him in reply, 'Lord, when did we see

---

[34] Adapted from the *Book of Blessings*, n. 202ff

you hungry and feed you, or thirsty and give you drink? When did we see you a stranger and make you welcome; naked and clothe you; sick or in prison and go to see you?' And the King will answer, 'I tell you solemnly, in so far as you did this to one of the least of these brothers of mine, you did it to me.'

Some intercessions may follow. If there are no intercessions, the minister invites those present to ask for God's help, in these or similar words:

My brothers and sisters, let us pray that God who is love will enkindle our hearts with the fire of the Holy Spirit, to give us an ardent love for others, like Christ's love for us.

As circumstances suggest, all may then pray for a moment in silence before the prayer of blessing. With hands outstretched, the minister continues with the prayer of blessing:

Blessed are you, Lord, God of mercy,
who through your Son gave us a marvellous example of charity
and the great commandment of love for one another.
Send down your blessings on these your servants,
who so generously devote themselves to helping others.
When they are called on in times of need,
let them faithfully serve you in their neighbour.
Through Christ our Lord.
R Amen.

BLESSING OF PILGRIMS[35]

In the name of the Father and of the Son and of the Holy Spirit.
R Amen.

One of those present, or the minister, reads a text of sacred scripture, for example:

Brothers and sisters, listen to the words of the gospel according to Matthew 8:18-22:

When Jesus saw the great crowds all about him he gave orders to leave for the other side. One of the scribes then came up and said to him, 'Master, I will follow you wherever you go.' Jesus replied, 'Foxes have holes and the birds of the air have nests, but the Son of Man has nowhere to lay his head.'

Another man, one of the disciples, said to him, 'Sir, let me go and bury my father first.' But Jesus replied, 'Follow me, and leave the dead to bury their dead.'

The minister says the prayer of blessing:

All-powerful God,
you always show mercy towards those who love you
and are never far away for those who seek you.
Remain with your servants on this holy pilgrimage
and guide their way in accord with your will.

---

[35] Adapted from the *Book of Blessings*, n. 595ff

Shelter them with your protection by day,
give the light of your grace by night,
and, as their companion on the journey,
bring them to their destination in safety.
Through Christ our Lord.
R Amen.

BLESSING OF THOSE
ON A JOURNEY[36]

In the name of the Father and of the Son and of the Holy Spirit.
R Amen.

One of those present, or the minister, reads a text of sacred scripture, for example:

Brothers and sisters, listen to the words of the book of Joshua 1:1,7-9:

Be strong and stand firm and be careful to keep all the Law which my servant Moses laid on you. Never swerve from this to right or left, and then you will be happy in all you do. Have the book of this Law always on your lips; meditate on it day and night, so that you may carefully keep everything that is written in it. Then you will prosper in your dealings, then you will have success. Have I not told you: Be strong and stand firm? Be fearless then, be confident, for go where you will, the Lord your God is with you.

Or

Matthew 8:23-27 *Jesus calms the storm*

Luke 24:13-35 *Jesus approached and began to walk with them*

John 14:1-11 *I am the way, the truth and the life*

---

[36] From the *Book of Blessings*, n. 620ff

A minister who is not going to accompany the travellers says the following prayer:

All-powerful God,
you led the children of Israel on dry land,
parting the waters of the sea;
you guided the Magi to your Son by a star.
Help these brothers and sisters
and give them a safe journey.
Under your protection let them reach their destination
and come at last to the eternal haven of salvation.
Through Christ our Lord.
R Amen.

A minister who is to accompany the travellers says the following prayer:

All-powerful and ever-living God,
when Abraham left his own land
and departed from his own people,
you kept him safe all through his journey.
Protect us, who also are your servants:
walk by our side to help us;
be our companion and our strength on the road
and our refuge in every adversity.
Lead us, O Lord,
so that we will reach our destination in safety
and happily return to our homes.
Through Christ our Lord.
R Amen.

BLESSINGS RELATED TO BUILDINGS AND TO VARIOUS FORMS OF HUMAN ACTIVITY

BLESSING OF A NEW HOME[37]

The blessing of a new home should only take place when at least some of those who will live in it are present.

In the name of the Father and of the Son and of the Holy Spirit.
R Amen.

One of those present, or the minister, reads a text of sacred scripture, for example:

Brothers and sisters, listen to the words of the holy gospel according to Luke 10:5-9:

The Lord said to the seventy-two: 'Whatever house you go into, let your first words be, "Peace to this house!" And if a man of peace lives there, your peace will go and rest on him; if not, it will come back to you. Stay in the same house, taking what food and

---

[37] Adapted from the *Book of Blessings*, n. 664ff

drink they have to offer, for the labourer deserves his wages; do not move about from house to house. Whatever you go into a town where they make you welcome, eat what is set before you. Cure those in it who are sick, and say, "The kingdom of God is very near to you."'

The minister says the prayer of blessing:

Lord,
be close to your servants
who move into this home (today)
and ask for your blessing.
Be their shelter when they are at home,
their companion when they are away,
and their welcome guest when they return.
And at last receive them into the dwelling place you have prepared for them
in your Father's house,
where you live for ever and ever.
R Amen.

After the prayer of blessing, the minister sprinkles those present and the home with holy water and, as circumstances suggest, may say:

Let this water call to mind our baptism into Christ, who has redeemed us by his death and resurrection.
R Amen.

The minister concludes the rite by saying:

May the peace of Christ rule in our hearts,
and may the word of Christ in all its richness dwell in us,
so that whatever we do in word and in work,
we will do in the name of the Lord.
R Amen.

As circumstances suggest, it is appropriate to place a Bible, crucifix, religious statue or icon in a permanent place of honour in the home before the rite concludes (see page 154 for the blessing of religious articles).

BLESSING OF A SCHOOL OR UNIVERSITY[38]

This order of blessing, which is for use by a priest or deacon, may be adapted for the blessing of new classrooms, school extensions etc. In most instances it may be preferable to have a fuller celebration than that given here. Thought would well be given to involving students, teachers and others who work in the building, as well as those involved in the financing and building work, in the various ministries involved in a festive celebration.

In the name of the Father and of the Son and of the Holy Spirit.
R Amen.

One of those present, or the minister, reads a text of sacred scripture, for example:

Brothers and sisters, listen to the words of the gospel according to John 8:28b, 29, 31-32:

Jesus said:

what the Father has taught me;
is what I preach
he who sent me is with me,
and has not left me to myself,
for I always do what pleases him ...

---

[38] Adapted from the *Book of Blessings*, n. 729ff

If you make my word your home
you will indeed be my disciples;
you will learn the truth,
and the truth will make you free.

Or

Matthew 11:25-30 *You have hidden these things from the learned and the clever and revealed them to children*

Before the prayer of blessing, some intercessions, composed to suit the occasion, may be included.

With hands outstretched, the minister says the prayer of blessing:

O God,
it is by your gracious favour
that today we inaugurate this work,
dedicated to education.
Grant that those who will come here as teachers or as students
may always pursue the truth
and learn to know you, the source of all truth.
Through Christ our Lord.
R Amen.

After the prayer of blessing, the minister sprinkles those present and the building with holy water. Meanwhile a suitable song may be sung.

With hands outstretched over those present, the minister concludes the rite by saying:

May the all-knowing God, who is Lord,
show us his ways;
may Christ, eternal Wisdom,
teach us the words of truth;
may the Holy Spirit, the blessed light,
always enlighten our minds,
so that we may learn what is right and good
and in our actions carry out what we have learned.
R Amen.

Then he blesses all present:
And may the blessing of almighty God,
the Father, and the Son, ✠ and the Holy Spirit,
come upon you and remain with you for ever.

BLESSING OF A PARISH CENTRE[39]

The blessing of a building for social and catechetical use in the parish may be given by the parish priest or by another priest or deacon delegated by him.

When the community has gathered, a suitable song may be sung.

In the name of the Father and of the Son and of the Holy Spirit.
R Amen.

The minister may greet those present with a familiar liturgical greeting and may briefly introduce the celebration.

One of those present, or the minister, reads a short text from sacred scripture, for example:

Brothers and sisters, listen to the words of the apostle Paul to the Ephesians 2:19-22:

So you are no longer aliens or foreign visitors: you are citizens like all the saints, and part of God's household. You are part of a building that has the apostles and prophets for its foundations, and Christ Jesus himself for its main cornerstone. As every structure is aligned on him, all grow into one holy temple in the Lord; and you too, in him, are being built into a house where God lives, in the Spirit.

---

[39] Adapted from the *Book of Blessings*, n. 770ff

The minister introduces the intercessions:

With praise and thanksgiving, let us ask God to bless this new parish centre.

Another person present continues:

Let us pray that all the baptised may renew their commitment to Christ. Lord, hear us.
R Lord, graciously hear us.

Let us pray that God will continue to bless the work of our parish. Lord, hear us. R

Let us pray for all who, by their work and contributions, helped to build this centre. Lord, hear us. R

Let us pray for all who will use this centre, that they may become more closely united within our community. Lord, hear us. R

The minister invites all present to pray the Lord's Prayer:

Jesus gathers us in faith and calls us to pray:

All: Our Father ...

The minister says the prayer of blessing with hands outstretched:

God of mercy and truth,
you sent your only Son
to be our Saviour and Lord.
He calls us together as his Church
to carry on the work of salvation.

We ask you now to bless us
and all who will use this parish hall (catechetical centre).
May all who come here know the presence of Christ,
experience the joy of his friendship,
and grow in his love.

Through Christ our Lord.
R Amen.

The minister concludes the rite by saying:

May the peace of Christ rule in your hearts,
and may the word of Christ dwell in you,
so that all that you do in word and in work,
you will do in the name of the Lord.
R Amen.

Then he blesses all present:

And may almighty God bless you all, the Father, and the Son, ✠ and the Holy Spirit.
R Amen.

BLESSING OF A CENTRE OF CARE FOR THE SICK[40]

This present order of blessing may be used by a priest or deacon. Since this blessing refers to those who care for the sick, it is important that at least some of those who will work as carers be present at the celebration.

In the name of the Father and of the Son and of the Holy Spirit.
R Amen.

One of those present, or the minister, reads a text of sacred scripture, for example:

Brothers and sisters, listen to the words of the holy gospel according to Matthew 4:23-25:

He went around the whole of Galilee teaching in their synagogues, proclaiming the Good News of the kingdom and curing all kinds of diseases and sickness among the people. His fame spread throughout Syria, and those who were suffering from diseases and painful complaints of one kind or another, the possessed, epileptics, the paralysed, were all brought to him, and he cured them. Large crowds followed him, coming from Galilee, the Decapolis, Jerusalem, Judea and Transjordania.

---

[40] Adapted from the *Book of Blessings*, n. 786ff

Or

Matthew 25:31-46 *I was ill and you comforted me*

Luke 10:30-37 *He was moved to pity at the sight of him*

With hands outstretched, the celebrant says the prayer of blessing:

Blessed are you, O God, our Father.
Through your Son you commanded your people
who walk in newness of life
to care compassionately for the sick.
Attend to the desires of your children.
By the grace of your Holy Spirit
make this place a house of blessing and a centre of love,
where physicians practice the art of healing wisely,
where nurses and aides serve the sick with care,
where the faithful come to visit Christ
in the person of their brothers and sisters.
Grant that, comforted in their illness,
the patients will quickly regain their health
and joyfully thank you
for the favours they have received.
Through Christ our Lord.

After the prayer of blessing, the celebrant sprinkles those present and the building with holy water as a suitable song is sung.

With hands outstretched over those present, the celebrant concludes the rite by saying:

God, the comforter of the afflicted and the strength of the weak,
has brought you together for the dedication of this building,
established for the care of the sick.
May he strengthen you by his grace,
so that, in serving the sick with tender charity,
you may serve Christ himself.
Who lives and reigns for ever and ever.
R Amen.

And may the blessing of almighty God, the Father, and the Son, ✠ and the Holy Spirit, come upon you and remain with you for ever.
R Amen.

ANNUAL BLESSING FOR USE IN CENTRES OF CARE FOR THE SICK

The celebration of such a blessing may be arranged by using elements in the rite of blessing given above, in combination with elements taken from the blessings of the sick, given on pages 70–84. In this way the celebration will make reference to both the sick and those who care for them.

BLESSING OF A CENTRE OF SOCIAL COMMUNICATION[41]

This present order of blessing may be used by a priest or deacon.

When the community has gathered, a suitable song may be sung.

In the name of the Father and of the Son and of the Holy Spirit.
R Amen.

The minister may greet those present with a familiar liturgical greeting and may briefly introduce the celebration.

One of those present, or the minister, reads a short text from sacred scripture, for example:

Brothers and sisters, listen to the words of the holy gospel according to Luke 4:16-21:

He came to Nazara, where he had been brought up, and went into the synagogue on the sabbath day as he usually did. He stood up to read, and they handed him the scroll of the prophet Isaiah. Unrolling the scroll he found the place where it is written:

The spirit of the Lord has been given to me,
for he has anointed me.

---

[41] Adapted from the *Book of Blessings*, n. 821ff

He has sent me to bring the good news to the poor,
to proclaim liberty to captives,
and to the blind new sight,
to set the downtrodden free,
to proclaim the Lord's year of favour!

He then rolled up the scroll, gave it back to the assistant and sat down. And all eyes in the synagogue were fixed on him. Then he began to speak to them. 'This text is being fulfilled today even as you listen.'

A responsorial psalm or another suitable song may follow. The minister may also give a brief explanation of the biblical text. As circumstances suggest, the blessing prayer that follows may be preceded by some intercessions. The intentions could refer to the wonder of scientific advance, the search for truth, the power of communication to unite, the need for wisdom, honesty and charity in communication.

With hands outstretched, the celebrant says the prayer of blessing:

Lord God almighty,
we humbly praise you,
for you enlighten and inspire
those who by probing the powers implanted in creation
develop the work of your hands in wonderful ways.
Look with favour on your servants
who use the technology discovered by long research.
Enable them to communicate truth,
to foster love, to uphold justice and right,
and to provide enjoyment.

Let them promote and support
that peace between peoples
which Christ the Lord brought from heaven,
for he lives and reigns with you for ever and ever.
R Amen.

After the prayer of blessing, the celebrant may
sprinkle those present and the place with holy water
as a suitable song is sung.

With hands outstretched over those present, the
celebrant may conclude the rite by saying:

May God, the Creator of all things,
who never ceases to work his wonders among us
enlighten our minds,
so that we may know him more deeply
and strive always to spread his truth and his peace.
R Amen.

And may almighty God bless you all,
the Father, and the Son, ✠ and the Holy Spirit.
R Amen.

The celebration may end with a suitable song.

BLESSING OF A CENTRE FOR SPORTS OR ATHLETICS[42]

In the name of the Father and of the Son and of the Holy Spirit.
R Amen.

One of those present, or the minister, reads a text of sacred scripture, for example:

Brothers and sisters, listen to the words of the first letter of Paul to the Corinthians 9:24-27:

All the runners at the stadium are trying to win, but only one of them gets the prize. You must run in the same way, meaning to win. All the fighters at the games go into strict training; they do this just to win a wreath that will wither away, but we do it for a wreath that will never wither. That is how I run, intent on winning; that is how I fight, not beating the air. I treat my body hard and make it obey me, for, having been an announcer myself, I should not want to be disqualified.

The minister says the prayer of blessing:

Lord, we sing your praises without ceasing.
You rule over all things with wonderful order,
you temper the cares and burdens of our toil,
and, by giving us rest and healthy recreation,
you refresh our weary bodies and minds.

---

[42] Adapted from the *Book of Blessings*, n. 838ff

We entreat your kindness,
that this place and its facilities
will contribute to leisure activities
that renew the spirit and strengthen mind and body.
Grant that all who meet here
may find the enrichment of companionship
and together offer you the praise that is your due.
Through Christ our Lord.
R Amen.

BLESSING OF A VEHICLE[43]

In the name of the Father and of the Son and of the Holy Spirit.
R Amen.

One of those present, or the minister, reads a short text from sacred scripture, for example, Matthew 22:37, 39, 40:

Jesus said:

'*You must love the Lord, your God, with all your heart … You must love your neighbour as yourself.* On these two commandments hang the whole Law, and the Prophets also.'

The minister says the prayer of blessing:

All-powerful God,
Creator of heaven and earth,
in the rich depths of your wisdom
you have empowered us to produce great and beautiful works.
Grant, we pray, that those who use this vehicle
may travel safely, with care for the safety of others.
Whether they travel for business or pleasure,
let them always find Christ to be the companion of their journey,
who lives and reigns for ever and ever.
R Amen.

---

[43] Adapted from the *Book of Blessings*, n. 873ff

BLESSING OF AN AIRCRAFT[44]

In the name of the Father and of the Son and of the Holy Spirit.
R Amen.

One of those present, or the minister, reads a short text from sacred scripture, for example, John 14:6:

Jesus said, 'I am the Way and the Truth and the Life. No one can come to the Father except through me.'

The minister then says the prayer of blessing:

Lord our God,
you walk on the wings of the wind
and the heavens declare your glory.
We bless you and proclaim your greatness in all your works.
In the richness of your wisdom
you have empowered us to create great and beautiful works.
Grant, we pray, that this airplane will serve to spread your praises
and contribute to the well-being of those who fly in it.
Through your blessing may its pilots and crew
operate it with prudence,
so that its passengers may reach their destination happily and safely.
Through Christ our Lord.
R Amen.

---

[44] Adapted from the *Book of Blessings*, n. 873ff

As circumstances suggest, the minister may sprinkle those present and the vehicle with holy water.

BLESSING OF A BOAT[45]

In the name of the Father and of the Son and of the Holy Spirit.
R Amen.

One of those present, or the minister, reads a text of sacred scripture, for example:

Brothers and sisters, listen to the words of the holy gospel according to Matthew 8:23-27:

Then he got into the boat followed by his disciples. Without warning a storm broke over the lake, so violent that the waves were breaking right over the boat. But he was asleep. So they went to him and woke him, saying, 'Save us, Lord, we are going down!' And he said to them, 'Why are you so frightened, you men of little faith?' And with that he stood up and rebuked the winds and the sea; and all was calm again. The men were astounded and said, 'Whatever kind of man is this? Even the winds and the sea obey him.'

The minister says the prayer of blessing:

God of boundless love,
at the beginning of creation
your Spirit hovered over the deep.
You called forth every creature,
and the seas teemed with life.

---

45 Adapted from the *Book of Blessings*, n. 881ff

Through your Son, Jesus Christ,
you have given us the rich harvest of salvation.

Bless this boat, its equipment and all who will use it.
Protect them from the dangers of wind and rain
and all the perils of the deep.
May Christ, who calmed the storm
and filled the nets of his disciples,
bring us all to the harbour of light and peace.

Grant this through Christ our Lord.
R Amen.

BLESSING OF A
COMPUTER CENTRE[46]

In the name of the Father and of the Son and of the Holy Spirit.
R Amen.

One of those present, or the minister, reads a text of sacred scripture, for example:

Brothers and sisters, listen to the words of the book of Wisdom 7:15-17, 21:

May God grant me to speak as he would wish
and express thoughts worthy of his gifts,
since he himself is the guide of Wisdom,
since he directs the sages.
We are indeed in his hand, we ourselves and our words,
with all our understanding, too, and technical knowledge.
It was he who gave me true knowledge of all that is,
who taught me the structure of the world and the properties of the elements ...
All that is hidden, all that is plain, I have come to know,
instructed by Wisdom who designed them all.

---

[46] Adapted from the *Book of Blessings*, n. 903ff

The minister says the prayer of blessing:

Blessed are you, Lord our God,
and worthy of all praise,
for you have provided for the perfecting of your creation
through human labour and intelligence,
and you show your own power and goodness
in the inventions of the human race.
Grant that all those who use this centre and its equipment to improve their lives
may recognise that you are wonderful in your works
and may learn to carry out your will more readily.
Through Christ our Lord.
R Amen.

BLESSING OF TOOLS OR OTHER EQUIPMENT FOR WORK[47]

In the name of the Father and of the Son and of the Holy Spirit.

R Amen.

One of those present, or the minister, reads a text of sacred scripture, for example, Thessalonians 3:7-8:

You know how you are supposed to imitate us: now we were not idle when we were with you, nor did we ever have our meals at anyone's table without praying for them; no, we worked night and day, slaving and straining, so as not to be a burden on any of you.

Or

Exodus 35:30-36 *God filled them with the skill and perception to carry out all that was required*

Matthew 13:1-9 *A sower went out to sow*

Luke 5:3-11 *If you say so, I will lower the nets*

---

[47] Adapted from the *Book of Blessings*, n. 924ff

With hands joined, the minister says the prayer of blessing:

In your loving providence, O God,
you have made the forces of nature
subject to the work of our hands.
Grant that by devotion to our own work
we may gladly cooperate with you
in the building up of creation.
Through Christ our Lord.
R Amen.

After the prayer of blessing, as circumstances suggest, the minister may sprinkle those present and the implements with holy water.

BLESSING OF ANIMALS[48]

In the name of the Father and of the Son and of the Holy Spirit.
R Amen.

One of those present, or the minister, reads a text of sacred scripture, for example:

Brothers and sisters, listen to the words of the book of Genesis 1:1, 24-27:

In the beginning, when God created the heavens and the earth ... God said, 'Let the earth produce every kind of living creature: cattle, reptiles and every kind of wild beast.' And so it was. God made every kind of wild beast, every kind of cattle, and every kind of land reptile. God saw that it was good. God said, 'Let us make man in our image, in the likeness of ourselves, and let them be masters of the fish of the sea, the birds of heaven, the cattle, all the wild beasts and all the reptiles that crawl upon the earth.'

God created man in the image of himself,
in the image of God he created him;
male and female he created them.

---

[48] Adapted from the *Book of Blessings*, n. 946ff

The minister says the prayer of blessing:

O God,
you have done all things wisely;
in your goodness you have made us in your image
and given us care over other living things.

Reach out with your right hand
and grant that these animals may serve our needs
and that your bounty in the resources of this life
may move us to seek more confidently
the goal of eternal life.
Through Christ our Lord.
R Amen.

After the prayer of blessing the minister may sprinkle those present and the animals with holy water.

The minister concludes the rite by saying:

May God, who created the animals of this earth as a help to us,
continue to protect and sustain us
with the grace his blessing brings,
now and for ever.
R Amen.

BLESSING OF FIELDS
AND FLOCKS[49]

In the name of the Father and of the Son and of the Holy Spirit.
R Amen.

One of those present, or the minister, reads a text of sacred scripture, for example:

Brothers and sisters, listen to the words of the book of Genesis 1:29-32a:

God said, 'Look, to you I give all the seed-bearing plants everywhere on the surface of the earth, and all the trees with seed-bearing fruit; this will be your food. And to all the wild animals, all the birds of heaven and all the living creatures that creep along the ground, I give all the foliage of the plants as their food.' And so it was. God saw all that he had made, and indeed it was very good.

The minister says the prayer of blessing:

O God,
from the very beginning of time you commanded
the earth to bring forth vegetation
and fruit of every kind.
You provide the sower with seed and give bread to eat.

---

[49] Adapted from the *Book of Blessings*, n. 970ff

Grant, we pray, that this land,
enriched by your bounty and cultivated by human hands,
may be fertile with abundant crops.
Then your people, enriched by the gifts of your goodness,
will praise you unceasingly now and for ages unending.
Through Christ our Lord.
R Amen.

BLESSING OF SEEDS AT PLANTING TIME[50]

In the name of the Father and of the Son and of the Holy Spirit.
R Amen.

One of those present, or the minister, reads a text of sacred scripture, for example:

Brothers and sisters, listen to the holy gospel according to Mark 4:26-29:

Jesus said to his disciples, 'This is what the kingdom of God is like. A man scatters seed on the land. Night and day, while he sleeps, when he is awake, the seed is sprouting and growing; how, he does not know. Of its own accord the land produces first the shoot, then the ear, then the full grain in the ear. And when the crop is ready, at once he starts to reap because the harvest has come.'

The minister says the prayer of blessing:

Lord of the harvest,
you placed the gifts of creation in our hands
and called us to till the earth and make it fruitful.
We ask your blessing
as we prepare to place these seeds in the earth.

---

[50] Adapted from the *Book of Blessings*, n. 989ff

May the care we show these seeds
remind us of your tender love for your people.
Through Christ our Lord.
R Amen.

BLESSING ON THE OCCASION OF THANKSGIVING FOR THE HARVEST[51]

This celebration may include a symbolic offering of first fruits of the harvest to God in thanksgiving for his gifts.

In the name of the Father and of the Son and of the Holy Spirit.
R Amen.

One of those present, or the minister, reads a text of sacred scripture, for example:

Brothers and sisters, listen to the words of the prophet Joel 2:21-24, 26:

O soil, do not be afraid;
be glad, rejoice,
for the Lord has done great things.

Beasts of the field, do not be afraid;
the pastures on the heath are green again,
the trees bear fruit,
vine and fig tree yield abundantly.

Sons of Zion, be glad
rejoice in the Lord your God;
for he has given you
the autumn rain, since he is just,
and has poured the rains down for you,
the autumn and spring rain, as before.

---

[51] Adapted from the *Book of Blessings*, n. 370ff

The threshing-floors will be full of grain,
the vats overflow with wine and oil ...

You will eat to your heart's content, will eat your fill,
and praise the name of the Lord your God
who has treated you so wonderfully.

The minister says:

Let us pray.

All may pray for a moment of silence before the prayer
of blessing. Alternatively, the invitation 'Let us pray'
and the moment of silent prayer may be replaced by
some intercessions, introduced by the minister.

The minister says the prayer of blessing:

God our Creator,
who never cease to bestow your bounteous fruits
from the rains of the heavens and the riches of the soil,
we thank your loving majesty for this year's harvest.
Through these blessings of your generosity
you have fulfilled the hopes of your children.
Grant that together they may praise your mercy
without end
and in their life amid the good things of this world
strive also after the blessings of the world to come.
Through Christ our Lord.
R Amen.

Or

All-powerful God,
we appeal to your tender care that
even as you temper the winds and rains
to nurture the fruits of the earth
you will also send upon them
the gentle shower of your blessing.
Fill the hearts of your people with gratitude,
that from the earth's fertility
the hungry may be filled with good things
and the poor and needy proclaim the glory of your
name.
Through Christ our Lord.
R Amen.

Facing those present, the minister concludes the rite
by saying:

Let us bless God,
for ever let us praise and extol the name
of Father, Son, and Holy Spirit.
R Amen.

BLESSING OF AN
ATHLETIC EVENT[52]

In the name of the Father and of the Son and of the Holy Spirit.
R Amen.

One of those present, or the minister, reads a text of sacred scripture, for example:

Brothers and sisters, listen to the words of the first letter of Paul to the Corinthians 9:24-27:

All the runners at the stadium are trying to win, but only one of them gets the prize. You must run in the same way, meaning to win. All the fighters at the games go into strict training; they do this just to win a wreath that will wither away, but we do it for a wreath that will never wither. That is how I run, intent on winning; that is how I fight, not beating the air. I treat my body hard and make it obey me, for, having been an announcer myself, I should not want to be disqualified.

The minister says the prayer of blessing:

Strong and faithful God,
as we come together for this contest,
we ask you to bless these athletes.

---

[52] Adapted from the *Book of Blessings*, n. 1024ff

Keep them safe from injury and harm,
instil in them respect for each other
and reward them for their perseverance.

Lead us all to the rewards of your kingdom
where you live and reign for ever and ever.
R Amen.

BLESSING BEFORE AND AFTER MEALS[53]

Before Meals
Bless us, O Lord, and these your gifts
which we are about to receive from your goodness.
Through Christ our Lord.
R Amen.

Or

Blessed are you, almighty Father,
who give us our daily bread.
Blessed is your only begotten Son,
who continually feeds us with the word of life.
Blessed is the Holy Spirit,
who brings us together at this table of love.
Blessed be God now and for ever.
R Amen.

After Meals
We give you thanks for all your gifts, almighty God,
living and reigning now and for ever.
R Amen.

Or

We give you thanks, holy Lord, our Father,
for your loving gifts of our food and drink.
Grant that some day we may sit at the table of your
heavenly kingdom
and there sing a hymn of praise to you for ever.
R Amen.

---

[53] Adapted from the *Book of Blessings*, n. 1030ff

Verses for Use During the Liturgical Year

Advent
Give ear, O Lord and shepherd of your people.
R Stir up your power and come.

Christmas
The Word became flesh, alleluia.
R And dwelt among us, alleluia.

Lent
No one lives on bread alone.
R But on every word that comes from the mouth of God.

Holy Thursday, Good Friday, Holy Saturday
For our sake Christ was obedient, accepting even death.
R Death on a cross.

Easter Week
This is the day the Lord has made, alleluia.
R Let us rejoice and be glad, alleluia.

Eastertide
The disciples recognised the Lord, alleluia.
R In the breaking of the bread, alleluia.

BLESSINGS OF OBJECTS THAT ARE DESIGNED OR ERECTED FOR USE IN CHURCHES, EITHER IN THE LITURGY OR IN POPULAR DEVOTIONS

BLESSING OF AN ORGAN[54]

It is envisaged that the organ is played publicly for the first time only after it is blessed. This suggests that any songs in this rite which occur before the prayer of blessing are best sung unaccompanied, or accompanied by an instrument other than the one to be blessed.

Order of Blessing
When the community has gathered, a suitable song may be sung.

In the name of the Father and of the Son and of the Holy Spirit.
R Amen.

The ministers greets those present using the words that follow, or using a greeting which is more familiar to those present.

---

[54] Adapted from the *Book of Blessings*, n. 1328ff

May the Lord, whose praises are sung by the saints, be with you all.
R And with your spirit.

The minister may briefly prepare those present for the blessing with some introductory words.

A reader, another person present or the minister reads a text of sacred scripture, for example:

Brothers and sisters, listen to the words of the apostle Paul to the Colossians 3:16-17:

Let the message of Christ, in all its richness, find a home with you. Teach each other, and advise each other, in all wisdom. With gratitude in your hearts sing psalms and hymns and inspired songs to God; and never say or do anything except in the name of the Lord Jesus, giving thanks to God the Father through him.

As circumstances suggest, the following responsorial psalm may be sung or said, or some other suitable song.

R Sing and shout for joy to the Lord.

All you peoples, clap your hands,
shout to God with cries of gladness,
For the Lord, the Most High, the awesome,
is the great king over all the earth. R

Sing praise to God, sing praise;
sing praise to our king, sing praise.

For king of all the earth is God;
sing hymns of praise. R

As circumstances suggest, the prayer of blessing may be preceded by the following or other more suitable intercessions:

Let us pray to the Lord, with thanksgiving in our hearts.

That the gift of music may deepen our appreciation of God's holy word: We pray to the Lord.
R Lord, hear our prayer.

That the words we sing may find a deep echo in our minds and hearts: We pray to the Lord. R

That we may sing to the Lord not only with our voices but with lives of love and adoration: We pray to the Lord. R

That our musicians may lead and support us in the joyful task of praising God: We pray to the Lord. R

That, united in song, we may become more united in worship and in daily living: We pray to the Lord. R

If there are no intercessions, the minister, before the prayer of blessing, invites those present to pray, in these or similar words:

Gathered together by the Holy Spirit as members of Christ's body, let us call upon God in voice and heart.

After a brief pause for silent prayer, the minister says the prayer of blessing:

Lord God,
your beauty is ancient yet ever new,
your wisdom guides the world in right order,
and your goodness gives the world its variety and splendour.
The choirs of angels join together
to offer their praise by obeying your commands.
The galaxies sing your praises by the pattern of their movement
that follows your laws.
The voices of the redeemed join in a chorus of praise to your holiness
as they sing to you in mind and heart.
We your people, joyously gathered in this church,
wish to join our voices to the universal hymn of praise.
So that our song may rise more worthily to your majesty,
we present this organ for your blessing:
grant that its music may lead us to express our prayer and praise
in melodies that are pleasing to you.
Through Christ our Lord.
R Amen.

Then the celebrant places incense in the censer and incenses the organ, as the organ is played for the first time.[55]

---

[55] It is not advisable to sprinkle such instruments with holy water.

With hands outstretched over the people, the celebrant blesses them by saying:

The Lord is worthy of all praise;
may he give you the gift of striving to sing a new song to him
with your voices, your hearts, and your lives,
so that one day you may sing that song for ever in heaven.
R Amen.

Then he blesses all present:

And may almighty God bless your all, the Father, and the Son, ✠ and the Holy Spirit.
R Amen.

BLESSINGS OF ARTICLES MEANT TO FOSTER THE DEVOTION OF THE CHRISTIAN PEOPLE

BLESSING OF RELIGIOUS ARTICLES[56]

This order of blessing is for the blessing of medals, small crucifixes, statues or pictures and other articles of personal devotion, and is for use by a priest or deacon.

In the name of the Father and of the Son and of the Holy Spirit.
R Amen.

One of those present, or the minister, reads a text of sacred scripture, for example:

Let us listen to the words of the holy gospel according to Luke 11:9-10:

So I say to you: Ask, and it will be given to you; search, and you will find; knock, and the door will be opened to you. For the one who asks always receives; the one who searches always finds; the one who knocks will always have the door opened to him.

---

[56] Adapted from the *Book of Blessings*, n. 1446ff

The minister says:

Let us pray.

As circumstances suggest, all may then pray for a moment in silence before the prayer of blessing.

With hands outstretched, the minister says the prayer of blessing:

Blessed be your name, O Lord,
you are the fount and source of every blessing,
and you look with delight
upon the devout practices of the faithful.
Draw near, we pray, to these your servants
and, as they use this symbol of their faith and devotion,
grant that they may also strive to be transformed
into the likeness of Christ, your Son,
who lives and reigns with you for ever and ever.
R Amen.

The minister concludes the rite by saying:

May God, who has revealed his glory to us in Christ,
bring your lives into conformity with the image of his Son,
so that you may reach the vision of his glory.
R Amen.

And may almighty God bless you, the Father, and the Son, ✠ and the Holy Spirit.
R Amen.

In special circumstances, a priest or deacon may use the following short blessing formulary for a single article:

May this name of article and the one who uses it be blessed,
in the name of the Father, and the Son, ✠ and the Holy Spirit.
R Amen.

BLESSING OF ROSARIES[57]

This order of blessing is for use by a priest or deacon. When a large number of rosaries are to be blessed, it is preferable that this occur in a celebration that precedes the recitation of the rosary in which the people take part.

In the name of the Father and of the Son and of the Holy Spirit.
R Amen.

One of those present, or the minister, reads a text of sacred scripture, for example, Acts 1:14:

All these joined in continuous prayer, together with several women, including Mary the mother of Jesus, and with his brothers.

With hands outstretched, the minister says the prayer of blessing:

Blessed be our God and Father,
who has given us the mysteries of his Son
to be pondered with devotion and celebrated with faith.
May he grant us, his faithful people,
that by praying the rosary
we may, with Mary the Mother of Jesus,
seek to keep his joys, sorrows and glories
in our minds and hearts.
Through Christ our Lord.
R Amen.

---

[57] Adapted from the *Book of Blessings*, n. 1482ff

In special circumstances a priest or deacon may use the following short blessing formulary:

May this rosary and the one who uses it be blessed, in the name of the Father, and the Son, ✠ and the Holy Spirit.
R Amen.

BLESSINGS RELATED TO FEASTS AND SEASONS

BLESSING OF AN ADVENT WREATH[58]

Two forms of blessing are included here. The first form is for use within Mass. The second is a shorter form which is particularly suitable for use in the family home. Suggestions are given as to how this may be adapted for use in other contexts. The wreath may also be blessed during Evening Prayer, and it is suggested that the Prayer of Blessing be said after the Short Responsory.

Once the Advent wreath has been blessed for use in church, on subsequent occasions the candles are lit for use at Mass either before Mass begins or before the Collect. When the Advent wreath is used at home it is suitable to recite the Collect of the Sunday Mass when the candles are lighted.

The Advent wreath may be blessed by a priest, deacon, or a lay minister. In the family home it is appropriate that it be blessed by a parent or another member of the family.

---

[58] Adapted from the *Book of Blessings*, n. 1509ff

Blessing Within Mass

The prayer of blessing forms the conclusion to the general intercessions. With hands outstretched, the celebrant says:

Lord our God,
we praise you for your Son, Jesus Christ:
he is Emmanuel, the hope of the peoples,
he is the wisdom that teaches and guides us,
he is the Saviour of every nation.

Lord God,
let your blessing come upon us
as we light the candles of this wreath.
May the wreath and its light
be a sign of Christ's promise to bring us salvation.
May he come quickly and not delay.
Through Christ our Lord.
R Amen.

The first candle is then lit.

Shorter Rite[59]

In the name of the Father and of the Son and of the Holy Spirit.
R Amen.

One of those present or the minister reads a text of sacred scripture, for example:

Brothers and sisters, listen to the words of the prophet Isaiah 9:1-6:

---

[59] Adapted from the *Book of Blessings*, n. 1537ff

The people that walked in darkness
have seen a great light;
on those who live in a land of deep shadow
a light has shone ...

For there is a child born for us,
a son given to us
and dominion is laid on his shoulders;
and this is the name they give him:
Wonder-Counsellor, Mighty-God,
Eternal-Father, Prince-of-Peace.

The minister says the prayer of blessing:

Lord our God,
we praise you for your Son, Jesus Christ:
he is Emmanuel, the hope of the peoples,
he is the wisdom that teaches and guides us,
he is the Saviour of every nation.

Lord God,
let your blessing come upon us
as we light the candles of this wreath.
May the wreath and its light
be a sign of Christ's promise to bring us salvation.
May he come quickly and not delay.
We ask this through Christ our Lord.
R Amen.

BLESSING OF THE
CHRISTMAS CANDLE

In the name of the Father and of the Son and of the
Holy Spirit.
R Amen.

One of those present, or the minister, reads a text of
sacred scripture, for example:

Brothers and sisters, listen to the words of the prophet
Isaiah 9:1-6:

The people that walked in darkness
have seen a great light;
on those who live in a land of deep shadow
a light has shone …

For there is a child born for us,
a son given to us
and dominion is laid on his shoulders;
and this is the name they give him:
Wonder-Counsellor, Mighty-God,
Eternal-Father, Prince-of-Peace.

If this scripture passage has already been used for the
blessing of the Advent wreath, an alternative text would
be John 1:6-10 *The real light which gives light to everyone.*

Let us pray with faith and devotion on this holy night:

May this candle shine as a light of welcome for those
who are homeless and in need.
R Glory to God, and peace on earth!

May those who are in trouble this night know God's care through the prayers of the Blessed Virgin Mary and Saint Joseph. R

May God bless our absent relatives and friends, especially N.. R

May eternal light shine on all who have died, especially N.. R

God of power
who enlightens the world
and dispels the darkness of ignorance and sin,
as we celebrate the birth of our Saviour
let the light of this candle
illumine our hearts and minds
that they may reflect always the splendour of Christ,
who is Lord, for ever and ever.
R Amen.

The candle is lit. 'Silent Night' or another well-known Christmas carol may be sung. For an additional Christmas prayer drawn from the Irish tradition, see page 237.

BLESSING OF A CHRISTMAS MANGER OR NATIVITY SCENE[60]

In the name of the Father and of the Son and of the Holy Spirit.
R Amen.

One of those present, or the minister, reads a text of sacred scripture, for example:

Brothers and sisters, listen to the words of the holy gospel according to Luke 2:1-8:

Now at this time Caesar Augustus issued a decree for a census of the whole world to be taken. This census – the first – took place while Quirinius was governor of Syria, and everyone went to his own town to be registered. So Joseph set out from the town of Nazareth in Galilee and travelled up to Judea, to the town of David called Bethlehem, since he was of David's house and line, in order to be registered together with Mary, his betrothed, who was with child. While they were there the time came for her to have her child, and she gave birth to a son, her first-born. She wrapped him in swaddling clothes and laid him in a manger because there was no room for them at the inn. In the countryside close by there were shepherds who lived in the fields and took it in turns to watch their flocks during the night.

---

[60] Adapted from the *Book of Blessings*, n. 1547ff

The minister says the prayer of blessing:

God of every nation and people,
from the very beginning of creation
you have made manifest your love:
when our need for a Saviour was great
you sent your Son to be born of the Virgin Mary.
To our lives he brings joy and peace,
justice, mercy, and love.
Lord, bless all who look upon this manger;
may it remind us of the humble birth of Jesus,
and raise up our thoughts to him,
who is God-with-us and Saviour of all,
and who lives and reigns for ever and ever.
R Amen.

BLESSING OF A CHRISTMAS TREE[61]

While the secular use of the Christmas tree is fairly modern, its religious use as a Christian symbol originates in medieval mystery plays. The tree and its lights can become a means of opening up to the symbolism of the tree of life in paradise, the tree of the cross, the lineage, or family tree, of Jesus and the light which comes into the world. The decoration of the tree should be in keeping with its use in church. Care should be taken that its position not distract in any way from the principal symbolic focus points of the sanctuary.

A Christmas tree in the home may also be blessed by a parent or other family member.

The rite of blessing begins with the lights of the tree unlit.

In the name of the Father and of the Son and of the Holy Spirit.
R Amen.

One of those present, or the minister, reads a text of sacred scripture, for example:

Brothers and sisters, listen to the words of the prophet Isaiah 9:1, 5:

**The people that walked in darkness
have seen a great light;
on those who live in a land of deep shadow
a light has shone ...**

---

[61] Adapted from the *Book of Blessings*, n. 1576ff

For there is a child born for us,
a son given to us
and dominion is laid on his shoulders;
and this is the name they give him:
Wonder-Counsellor, Mighty-God,
Eternal-Father, Prince-of-Peace.

The minister says the prayer of blessing:

Lord our God,
we praise you for the light of creation:
the sun, the moon, and the stars of the night.
We praise you for the light of Israel:
the Law, the prophets, and the wisdom of the
scriptures.
We praise you for Jesus Christ, your Son:
he is Emmanuel, God-with-us, the Prince of Peace,
who fills us with the wonder of your love.

Lord God,
let your blessing come upon us
as we illumine this tree.
May the light and cheer it gives
be a sign of the joy that fills our hearts.
May all who delight in this tree
come to the knowledge and joy of salvation.
Through Christ our Lord.
R Amen.

The lights of the tree are lit. Meanwhile a hymn such as 'O Come, O Come, Emmanuel' is sung, or the following acclamations are used:

Lord Jesus, Son of God and Son of Mary.
R We welcome you, O Lord.

Lord Jesus, hope of the shepherds and the poor.
R We welcome you, O Lord.

Lord Jesus, glory of the angels.
R We welcome you, O Lord.

BLESSING OF A JESSE TREE[62]

In the name of the Father and of the Son and of the Holy Spirit.
R Amen.

One of those present, or the minister, reads a text of sacred scripture, for example:

Let us listen to the words of St Paul's letter to the Romans 9:4-5:

They were adopted as sons, they were given the glory and the covenants; the Law and the ritual were drawn up for them, and the promises were made to them. They are descended from the patriarchs and from their flesh and blood came Christ who is above all, God for ever blessed! Amen.

The minister introduces the intercessions:

Let us ask God's blessing in this holy season of Advent, that pondering on the ways of God's mercy, from one generation to the next, we may praise the Lord's goodness.

Remembering Abraham and Sarah, may we grow in faith.
R Lord, send us your blessing.

Remembering Moses, Miriam, Isaiah and all the prophets, may we hear and live God's word. R

---

[62] Adapted from the *Book of Blessings*, n. 1786ff

Remembering David and the holy kings of Israel, may we allow God's love to reign in our hearts. R

Remembering John, who prepared the way for Jesus, may we recognise the Lamb of God among us. R

Remembering, above all, Mary, the Holy Mother of God, and St Joseph, may we welcome the Word made flesh among us. R

The minister says the prayer of blessing:

Lord God,
you beautify your Church
with the rich variety of the virtues of your saints.
Show your kindness to these your servants,
who with devotion wish to use this sign of your goodness.
Grant that they may be filled with the love of your commandments
and that, sustained by the helps they need in the present life,
they may progress toward the goal of life everlasting.
Through Christ our Lord.
R Amen.

The Jesse tree may now be sprinkled with holy water.

BLESSING OF THROATS ON THE FEAST OF ST BLAISE[63]

The blessing of throats may be given by a priest, deacon, or a lay minister. The blessing is given individually with two candles held in the form of a cross to the throat of each person. Often the candles will have been blessed on the previous day as part of the celebration of the Presentation of the Lord. If the blessing is given during Mass it follows the general intercessions or may take the place of the final blessing of the Mass. If the numbers attending Mass are so large that individual blessings are not possible, the celebrant says the prayer of blessing while extending hands over the entire congregation. If the blessing is celebrated at Morning Prayer or Evening Prayer, it is given before the gospel canticle. In other circumstances the blessing is given in the context of a liturgy of the word.

Prayer of Blessing

A priest or deacon makes the sign of the cross while saying the prayer of blessing.

Through the intercession of Saint Blaise, bishop and martyr, may God deliver you from every disease of the throat and from every other illness:

In the name of the Father, and of the Son, ✠ and of the Holy Spirit.

Each person responds:

Amen.

---

[63] Adapted from the *Book of Blessings*, n. 1622ff.

Blessing During a Liturgy of the Word

In the name of the Father and of the Son and of the Holy Spirit.

R Amen.

One of those present, or the minister, reads a text of sacred scripture, for example:

Let us listen to the words of the holy gospel according to Matthew 8:14-17:

And going into Peter's house Jesus found Peter's mother-in-law in bed with fever. He touched her hand and the fever left her, and she got up and began to wait on him.

That evening they brought him many who were possessed by devils. He cast out the spirits with a word and cured all who were sick. This was to fulfil the prophecy of Isaiah:

He took our sicknesses away and carried our diseases for us.

The celebration continues with some intercessions. The Lord's Prayer is then recited or sung. The blessing is then given, as indicated above for use during Mass.

BLESSING OF EASTER FOOD[64]

In the name of the Father and of the Son and of the Holy Spirit.
R Amen.

One of those present, or the minister, reads a text of sacred scripture, for example:

Let us listen to the words of the holy gospel according to Luke 24:36-43:

They were still talking about all this when he himself stood among them and said to them, 'Peace be with you!' In a state of alarm and fright, they thought they were seeing a ghost. But he said, 'Why are you so agitated, and why are these doubts rising in your hearts? Look at my hands and my feet; yes, it is I indeed. Touch me and see for yourselves; a ghost has no flesh and bones as you can see I have.' And as he said this he showed them his hands and feet. Their joy was so great that they still could not believe it, and they stood there dumbfounded; so he said to them, 'Have you anything here to eat?' And they offered him a piece of grilled fish, which he took and ate before their eyes.

The minister says the prayer of blessing:

God of glory,
the eyes of all turn to you
as we celebrate Christ's victory over sin and death.

---

[64] Adapted from the *Book of Blessings*, n. 1707ff

Bless us and this food of our first Easter meal.
May we who gather at the Lord's table
continue to celebrate the joy of his resurrection
and be admitted finally to his heavenly banquet.
Through Christ our Lord.
R Amen.

BLESSING OF FOOD OR DRINK OR OTHER ELEMENTS (SUCH AS WATER, FLOWERS OR CANDLES)[65]

In the name of the Father and of the Son and of the Holy Spirit.
R Amen.

The minister may briefly prepare those present for the blessing with some introductory words.

A reader, another person present or the minister reads a text of sacred scripture, for example:

Brothers and sisters, listen to the words of the holy gospel according to Matthew 7:7-11:

Ask, and it will be given to you; search, and you will find; knock, and the door will be opened to you. For the one who asks always receives; the one who searches always finds; the one who knocks will always have the door opened to him. Is there a man among you who would hand his son a stone when he asked for bread? Or would hand him a snake when he asked for a fish? If you, then, who are evil, know how to give your children what is good, how much more will your Father in heaven give good things to those who ask him!

---

[65] Adapted from the *Book of Blessings*, n. 1781ff

Or

Blessing of water
Exodus 17:1-7   *Give us water to drink*

Blessing of bread
1 Kings 19:3b-8:   *Strengthened by that food, he walked forty days and forty nights*

Blessing of other foods
Genesis 9:1-3   *Every living and crawling thing shall provide food for you*

Blessing of oil, wine, salt
Matthew 5:13-16   *You are the salt of the earth*
Luke 10:30-37   *He dressed his wounds, pouring in oil and wine*

Blessing of flowers
Matthew 6:25-34   *Learn a lesson from the way the wild flowers grow*

Blessing of candles
Matthew 4:13-17   *The people have seen a great light*

The minister says the prayer of blessing:

A. Blessing of food
Blessed are you, Lord God,
who have showered all creatures with your blessings.
Hear the prayers of these your servants:
that whenever they eat this food (bread)
(in honour of the blessed Virgin Mary or Saint N.)

they may be blessed with your heavenly blessing; that
striving always for what is holy, they may continually
grow in charity.
Through Christ our Lord.
R Amen.

B. Blessing of wine

Blessed are you, Lord God,
who fill the hungry and satisfy the thirsty,
and give us wine to gladden our hearts.
Grant that all who drink this wine
(in remembrance of the blessed Virgin Mary or Saint
N.)
may rejoice in you
and be invited to sit at your heavenly banquet for ever
and ever.
R Amen.

C. Blessing of flowers

Lord God,
creator of all that is beautiful,
the splendour of these flowers reflects your glory.
As we gather together (on this feast of name of feast of
Mary or Saint N.),
we ask you to bless ✠ these flowers,
so that the faithful who use them to adorn their homes
(this church)
may praise you always for the beauty
with which you clothed your creation.
Through Christ our Lord.
R Amen.

D. Blessing of candles

God of power
who enlightens the world
and dispels the darkness of ignorance and sin,
(as we remember the Virgin Mother of your Son or
Saint N.)
let the light of these candles
illumine our hearts and minds
that they may reflect always the splendour of Christ,
who is Lord, for ever and ever.
R Amen.

E. Blessing of oil

God of compassion, mercy, and love,
in the midst of the pain and suffering of the world
your Son came among us
to heal our infirmities and soothe our wounds.
May all who use this oil (in honour of Saint N.)
be blessed with health of mind and body.
Through Christ our Lord.
R Amen.

F. Blessing of other materials

Lord God,
you beautify your Church with the rich variety of the
virtues of your saints.
Show your kindness to these your servants,
who with devotion wish to use this sign (these signs)
of your goodness
(in remembrance and in honour of the blessed Virgin
Mary or Saint N.).

Grant that they may be filled with the love of your commandments
and that, sustained by the help they need in the present life,
they may progress toward the goal of life everlasting.
Through Christ our Lord.
R Amen.

G. Blessing of several things at once
God of power and goodness,
source of all grace and crown of all the saints,
through the intercession of Mary (or Saint N.)
grant that as we use (the name of the things to be blessed) brought here for your blessing, we may be eager to imitate him/her
whose life we celebrate,
and that our reward in heaven may be the company of Mary (or Saint N.),
whose protection is our comfort on earth.
Through Christ our Lord.
R Amen.

If this is the local custom, the objects blessed may now be sprinkled with holy water.

BLESSINGS FOR VARIOUS NEEDS AND OCCASIONS

FOR READERS[66]

Blessing Within Mass

The general intercessions take place in the usual way during the Liturgy of the Word, and should include intercessions for the new readers. The prayer of blessing forms the conclusion to the intercessions. With hands extended over the new readers, the celebrant says:

Everlasting God,
when he read in the synagogue at Nazareth,
your Son proclaimed the good news of salvation
for which he would give up his life.

Bless these readers.
As they proclaim your words of life,
strengthen their faith
that they may read with conviction and boldness,
and put into practice what they read.

---

[66] Adapted from the *Book of Blessings*, n. 1827ff

Through Christ our Lord.
R Amen.

If desired, each new reader may be presented with a
lectionary or Bible after the prayer of blessing.

FOR ALTAR SERVERS, SACRISTANS, MUSICIANS AND USHERS[67]

Blessing Within Mass

The general intercessions take place in the usual way during the Liturgy of the Word, and should include intercessions for those on whom God's blessing is to be invoked. The prayer of blessing forms the conclusion to the intercessions. With hands extended over the new readers, the celebrant says:

God of glory,
your beloved Son has shown us
that true worship comes from humble and contrite hearts.

Bless our brothers and sisters,
who have responded to the needs of our parish
and wish to commit themselves to your service as
(altar servers, sacristans, musicians, ushers).
Grant that their ministry may be fruitful
and our worship pleasing in your sight.

Through Christ our Lord.
R Amen.

---

[67] Adapted from the *Book of Blessings*, n. 1853ff

FOR COMMISSIONING OF EXTRAORDINARY MINISTERS OF HOLY COMMUNION[68]

ORDER OF COMMISSIONING WITHIN MASS

After the gospel reading, the celebrant in the homily, based on the sacred text and pertinent to the particular place and the people involved, explains the meaning of the celebration.

Then he presents to the people those chosen to serve as special ministers, using these or similar words:

Dear friends in Christ, our brothers and sisters N. and N. are to be entrusted with administering the Eucharist, with taking communion to the sick, and with giving it as viaticum to the dying.

The celebrant pauses, and then addresses the candidates:

In this ministry you must be examples of Christian living in faith and conduct; you must strive to grow in holiness through this sacrament of unity and love. Remember that, though many, we are one body because we share the one bread and one cup.

As ministers of holy communion be, therefore, especially observant of the Lord's command to love your neighbour. For when he gave his body as food

---

[68] Taken from the *Book of Blessings*, n. 1874ff

to his disciples, he said to them: 'This is my commandment, that you should love one another as I have loved you.'

After the address the candidates stand before the celebrant, who asks them these questions:

Are you resolved to undertake the office of giving the body and blood of the Lord to your brothers and sisters, and so serve to build up the Church?
R I am.

Are you resolved to administer the holy Eucharist with the utmost care and reverence?
R I am.

All stand. The candidates kneel and the celebrant invites the faithful to pray:

Dear friends in Christ, let us pray with confidence to the Father; let us ask him to bestow his blessings on our brothers and sisters, chosen to be minister of the Eucharist.

Pause for silent prayer. The celebrant then continues:

Gracious Lord,
you nourish us with the body and blood of your Son,
that we might have eternal life.
Bless ✠ our brothers and sisters who have been chosen to give the bread of heaven and the cup of salvation to your faithful people.

May the saving mysteries they distribute
lead them to the joys of eternal life.

Through Christ our Lord.
R Amen.

The general intercessions follow.

In the procession at the presentation of gifts, the
newly commissioned ministers carry the vessels with
the bread and wine, and at communion may receive
the Eucharist under both kinds.

FOR THOSE WHO EXERCISE PASTORAL SERVICE[69]

This blessing, which may be given by a priest or a deacon, is for lay people as they begin to exercise service in the life of a parish.

Blessing Within Mass

After the homily, intercessions follow. Below is a sample which may be adapted.

The celebrant says:

Let us now ask God to strengthen and bless our brothers and sisters as they begin their new pastoral service in this parish.

An assisting minister continues:

That those who exercise pastoral service may grow to a greater love of Christ, let us pray to the Lord.
R Lord, hear our prayer.

That they may lighten the burdens of others and assist them in their struggles, let us pray to the Lord. R

That the Holy Spirit may strengthen their hearts and enlighten their minds, let us pray to the Lord. R

That through their endeavours, this parish may grow in faith, hope and love, let us pray to the Lord. R

---

[69] Adapted from the *Book of Blessings*, n. 1811ff

With hands extended over the new ministers, the celebrant says:

Lord God,
in your loving kindness
you sent your Son to be our shepherd and guide.
Continue to send workers into your vineyard
to sustain and direct your people.
Bless N. N. and N. N..
Let your Spirit uphold them always
as they take up their new responsibility
among the people of this parish.
Through Christ our Lord.
R Amen.

Blessing Within a Celebration of the Word of God

If the blessing takes place outside Mass, the intercessions and prayer of blessing should be preceded by a reading from sacred scripture, for example:

Matthew 5:1-12 *Rejoice, for your reward in heaven is great*

Jeremiah 1:4-9 *To whomever I send you, you shall go*

Romans 10:9-18 *How will they hear without someone preaching?*

Mark 16:15-20 *Go into the whole world and preach the gospel*

FOR STUDENTS SITTING
EXAMINATIONS[70]

In the name of the Father and of the Son and of the
Holy Spirit.
R Amen.

One of those present, or the minister, reads a text of
sacred scripture, for example:

Let us listen to the words of the holy gospel according
to Luke 2:46-48:

Three days later, they found him in the Temple, sitting
among the doctors, listening to them, and asking them
questions; and all those who heard him were
astounded at his intelligence and his replies.

The minister says:

God loves us and sustains us. Let us ask for his
blessing, praying that he will renew and support us
with his strength.

One of those present, or the minister, continues:

Everlasting God, pour out your spirit of wisdom on
these students.
R Lord, give us your blessing.

Help them to remain calm and to attend carefully to
the questions asked. R

---

[70] Adapted from the *Book of Blessings*, n. 1984ff

Help them to think clearly, to remember accurately, and to express themselves well. R

May they reflect the best of the work they have done, and the best of the teaching they have received. R

May your love be upon them O Lord, as they place all their trust in you. R
R Amen.

The minister says the prayer of blessing:

Lord,
let the effect of your blessing
remain with your faithful people
to give them new life and strength of spirit,
so that the power of your love
will enable them to accomplish what is right and good.

Through Christ our Lord.
R Amen.

FOR THOSE WHO CARE FOR
THE ELDERLY[71]

In the name of the Father and of the Son and of the Holy Spirit.
R Amen.

One of those present, or the minister, reads a text of sacred scripture, for example:

Brothers and sisters, listen to the words of the holy gospel according to Matthew 25:31-40:

Jesus said to his disciples:

'When the Son of Man comes in his glory, escorted by all the angels, then he will take his seat on his throne of his glory. All the nations will be assembled before him and he will separate men one from another as the shepherd separates sheep from goats. He will place the sheep on his right hand and the goats on his left. Then the King will say to those on his right hand, "Come, you whom my Father has blessed, take for your heritage the kingdom prepared for you since the foundation of the world. For I was hungry and you gave me food; I was thirsty and you gave me drink; I was a stranger and you made me welcome; naked and you clothed me, sick and you visited me, in prison and you came to see me." Then the virtuous will say to him in reply, "Lord, when did we see hungry and feed you; or thirsty and give you drink? When did we see you a stranger and make you welcome; naked and clothe

---

[71] Adapted from the *Book of Blessings*, n. 1984ff

you; sick or in prison and go to see you?" And the King will answer, "I tell you solemnly, in so far as you did it to one of the least of these brothers of mine, you did it to me."'

The minister says:

Let us pray that God will bestow his blessing upon us and that he will renew and support us with his strength.

One of those present, or the minister, continues:

Fill us with your Spirit, that we may nourish and refresh others.
R Lord, send us your blessing.

Fill us with you love, that we may give healing and support. R

Give us wisdom that we may see the face of Christ in all those whom we serve. R

Give us receptive hearts that recognise and welcome the gifts of others. R

The minister says the prayer of blessing:

Lord,
let the effect of your blessing
remain with your faithful people
to give them new life and strength of spirit,
so that the power of your love
will enable them to accomplish what is right and good.
Through Christ our Lord.
R Amen.

FOR CIVIC LEADERS[72]

In the name of the Father and of the Son and of the Holy Spirit.
R Amen.

One of those present, or the minister, reads a text of sacred scripture, for example:

Brothers and sisters, let us listen to the Book of Wisdom 9:1-4, 10-12a:

God of our ancestors, Lord of mercy,
who by your word have made all things,
and in your wisdom have fitted man
to rule the creatures that have come from you,
to govern the world in holiness and justice
and in honesty of soul to wield authority,
grant me Wisdom, consort of your throne,
and do not reject me from the number of your
children ...

Despatch her from the holy heavens,
send her forth from your throne of glory
to help me and to toil with me
and teach me what is pleasing to you,
since she knows and understands everything.
She will guide me prudently in my undertakings
and protect me by her glory.
Then all I do will be acceptable.

---

[72] Adapted from the *Book of Blessings*, n. 1984ff

God's love sustains the universe. Let us pray that he will bestow his blessing upon us and that he will renew and support us with his strength.

Give our civic leaders courage to follow noble aspirations for the good of all.
R Lord, send us your blessing.

Give them strength to support worthy causes. R

Give them integrity to seek the truth. R

Inspire and guide them in all their civic duties. R

Lord,
let the effect of your blessing
remain with your faithful people
to give them new life and strength of spirit,
so that the power of your love
will enable them to accomplish what is right and good.
Through Christ our Lord.
R Amen.

FOR THOSE WHO WORK IN THE COMMUNICATIONS MEDIA[73]

In the name of the Father and of the Son and of the Holy Spirit.
R Amen.

One of those present, or the minister, reads a text of sacred scripture, for example:

Brothers and sisters, let us listen to the words of St Paul in the Letter to the Romans 10:14-18:

But they will not ask his help unless they believe in him, and they will not believe in him unless they have heard of him, and they will not hear of him unless they get a preacher, and they will never have a preacher unless one is sent, but as scripture says: *The footsteps of those who bring good news is a welcome sound.* Not everyone, of course, listens to the Good News. As Isaiah says: *Lord, how many believed what we proclaimed?* So faith comes from what is preached, and what is preached comes from the word of Christ.

Let me put the question: is it possible that they did not hear? Indeed they did; in the words of the psalm, *their voice has gone out through all the earth, and their message to the ends of the world.*

---

[73] Adapted from the *Book of Blessings*, n. 1984ff. See also the Blessing of a Centre of Social Communication, p. 122.

The minister introduces the intercessions:

Let us pray to the Lord, who wants us all to be bound closely together in a union of truth and freedom.

The minister introduces the intercessions:

Let us pray to the Lord, who wants us all to be bound closely together in a union of truth and freedom.

One of those present, or the minister, continues:

Help us to use our talents with honesty, fairness and without prejudice.
R Lord, send us your blessing.

May we seek the truth and be fearless in exposing corruption. R

May we have a special concern for those who suffer and work for their relief. R

May our work serve the cause of peace and restore harmony where there is division. R

The minister says the prayer of blessing:

Lord,
let the effect of your blessing
remain with your faithful people
to give them new life and strength of spirit,
so that the power of your love
will enable them to accomplish what is right and good.
Through Christ our Lord.
R Amen.

FOR FINE WEATHER[74]

In the name of the Father and of the Son and of the Holy Spirit.
R Amen.

One of those present, or the minister, reads a text of sacred scripture, for example:

Brothers and sisters, let us listen to the Book of Ecclesiasticus 43:1-5:

Pride of heights, shining vault,
    So, in a glorious spectacle, the sky appears.
The sun, as he emerges, proclaims at his rising,
    'A thing of wonder is the work of the Most High!'
At his zenith he parches the ground,
    who can withstand his blaze?
A man must blow a furnace to produce any heat,
    the sun burns the mountains three times as much;
breathing out blasts of fire,
    flashing his rays he dazzles the eyes.
Great is the Lord who made him,
    and whose word speeds him on his course.

The minister introduces the intercessions:

God loves his creation and his goodness sustains the universe. Let us pray now that he will bestow his blessing upon us and that he will renew and support us with his strength.

---

[74] Adapted from the *Book of Blessings*, n. 1984ff

May the Lord bless farmers and all who work outdoors with the weather they need to provide for our welfare. R Lord, send us your blessing.

May the Lord refresh with fine weather those who need outdoor recreation and exercise. R

May the Lord teach us how to live in this world with respect for the delicate balance of climate. R

May the Lord help us to learn the lessons of the natural world, created as a space for our growth in body and spirit. R

The minister says the prayer of blessing:

Lord,
we, your people, pray for the gift of your holy blessing to ward off every harm and
to bring to fulfilment every right desire.
Through Christ our Lord.
R Amen.

FOR A JUBILEE OF RELIGIOUS PROFESSION[75]

In the name of the Father and of the Son and of the Holy Spirit.
R Amen.

One of those present, or the minister, reads a text of sacred scripture, for example:

Brothers and sisters, let us listen to the gospel according to Mark 10:28-31:

Peter took this up. 'What about us?' he asked him. 'We have left everything and followed you.' Jesus said, 'I tell you solemnly, there is no one who has left house, brothers, sisters, father, children or land for my sake and for the sake of the gospel who will not be repaid a hundred times over, houses, brothers, sisters, mothers, children and land – not without persecutions – now in this present time and, in the world to come, eternal life.

'Many who are first will be last, and the last first.'

The minister introduces the intercessions:

God loves his creation and his goodness sustains the universe. As we celebrate the jubilee of N., let us pray that he will renew his blessings and support us with his strength.

---

[75] Adapted from the *Book of Blessings*, n. 1984ff

Another person present, or the minister, continues:

God of faithfulness, as N. gives thanks to you today, may he/she rededicate that gift first received from you.
R Lord, send us your blessing.

Accept the offering of his/her loving service given to your people over many years. R

Renew within him/her the gift of loving dedication. R

May N.'s way of life give you glory in the years ahead. R

The minister says the prayer of blessing:

Lord God,
from the abundance of your mercy
enrich your servants and safeguard them.
Strengthened by your blessing,
may they always be thankful to you
and bless you with unending joy.
Through Christ our Lord.

The texts given here are of a general nature. They may be adapted, especially the choice of scripture text and the intercessions, to reflect more clearly the charisms of the religious life being celebrated.

FOR THOSE WHO ARE HOMELESS[76]

In the name of the Father and of the Son and of the Holy Spirit.
R **Amen.**

One of those present, or the minister, reads a text of sacred scripture, for example:

Brothers and sisters, let us listen to the gospel according to Matthew 8:19-20:

One of the scribes then came up and said to him, 'Master, I will follow you wherever you go.' Jesus replied, 'Foxes have holes and the birds of the air have nests, but the Son of man has nowhere to lay his head.'

Or

Brothers and sisters, let us listen to the gospel according to John 15:9-11:

Jesus said to his disciples,

As the Father has loved me,
so I have loved you.
Remain in my love.
If you keep my commandments
you will remain in my love,
just as I have kept my Father's commandments
and remain in his love.

---

[76] Adapted from the *Book of Blessings*, n. 1984ff

I have told you this
so that my own joy may be in you
and your joy be complete.

The minister introduces the intercessions:

Let us pray to God whose love sustains us on our journey through life.

Another person present, or the minister, continues:

Comfort us Lord with the knowledge that you love us, and help us to trust in your constant care.
R Lord, send us your blessing.

Inspire those in public office to provide adequate housing and accommodation for everyone. R

Make the Christian community a place of welcome where no one is left out. R

Train all of us into a spirit of solidarity and mutual support. R

The minister says the prayer of blessing:

Bless your people, Lord,
who wait for the gift of your compassion.
Grant that what they desire by your inspiration
they may receive through your goodness.
Through Christ our Lord.
R Amen.

FOR INNER HEALING[77]

In the name of the Father and of the Son and of the Holy Spirit.
R Amen.

One of those present, or the minister, reads a text of sacred scripture, for example:

Brothers and sisters, let us listen to the gospel according to Matthew 11:28-30:

Come to me, all you who labour and are overburdened, and I will give you rest. Shoulder my yoke and learn from me, for I am gentle and humble in heart, *and you will find rest for your souls*. Yes, my yoke is easy and my burden light.

The minister introduces the intercessions:

Let us place our trust in God's healing power, praying that he will renew and support us with his strength.

Another person present, or the minister, continues:

Touch the mind and heart of our brother/sister N..
R Lord, send us your blessing.

Fill him/her with the strength of your Holy Spirit. R

Free him/her from anxiety, guilt and distress. R

Enable him/her to turn to you in faith and love and to receive your peace and joy. R

---

[77] Adapted from the *Book of Blessings*, n. 1984ff

The minister says the prayer of blessing:

Lord,
let the effect of your blessing
remain with your faithful people
to give them new life and strength of spirit,
so that the power of your love
will enable them to accomplish what is right and good.
Through Christ our Lord.

The minister concludes the rite by saying:

May God, who is blessed above all,
bless you in all things through Christ,
so that whatever happens in your lives
will work together for your good.
R Amen.

A priest or deacon continues:

And may almighty God bless you, the Father, and the Son, ✠ and the Holy Spirit.
R Amen.

FOR A SITUATION OF LONELINESS[78]

In the name of the Father and of the Son and of the Holy Spirit.
R Amen.

A text of sacred scripture is read, for example:

Let us listen to the words of St Paul's letter to the Romans 8:35-37:

Nothing therefore can come between us and the love of Christ, even if we are troubled or worried, or being persecuted, or lacking food or clothes, or being threatened or even attacked. As scripture promised: *For your sake we are being massacred daily, and reckoned as sheep for the slaughter.* These are the trials through which we triumph, by the power of him who loved us.

The minister introduces the intercessions:

Let us pray to God, the source of all consolation.
R Lord, give us your blessing.

Another person, or the minister, continues:

In this time of loneliness assure us of the love of Christ. R

Be our companion each day, guiding us forward. R

Strengthen us with comfort and with hope for the future. R

---

[78] Adapted from the *Book of Blessings*, n. 1984ff

Fill our emptiness and nourish us in moments of weakness. R

The minister says the prayer of blessing:

Bless your people, Lord,
who wait for the gift of your compassion.
Grant that what they desire by your inspiration
they may receive through your goodness.
Through Christ our Lord.
R Amen.

FOR THOSE WHO SERVE IN THE CAUSE OF PEACE[79]

In the name of the Father and of the Son and of the Holy Spirit.
R Amen.

One of those present or the minister reads a text of sacred scripture, for example:

Brothers and sisters, listen to the holy gospel according to John 14:27:

Peace I bequeath to you,
my own peace I give you,
a peace the world cannot give, this is my gift to you.
Do not let your hearts be troubled or afraid.

The minister introduces the intercessions:

Let us pray in the name of Jesus, the Prince of Peace.

Another person present, or the minister, continues:

Bless all who serve in the cause of peace on land and sea and in the air.
R Lord, give us your blessing.

Help them to meet danger with courage and wisdom.
R

Help them to be models of discipline and loyalty. R

---

[79] Adapted from the *Book of Blessings*, n. 1984ff

May they strengthen the faint-hearted, support the weak and help the afflicted. R

May they work loyally to build up your kingdom of peace, love and justice. R

The minister says the prayer of blessing:

Lord,
let the effect of your blessing
remain with your faithful people
to give them new life and strength of spirit,
so that the power of your love
will enable them to accomplish what is right and good.
Through Christ our Lord.

The minister concludes the rite by saying:

May God, who is blessed above all,
bless you in all things through Christ,
so that whatever happens in your lives
will work together for your good.
R Amen.

A priest or deacon continues:

And may almighty God bless you, the Father, and the Son, ✠ and the Holy Spirit.
R Amen.

FOR A PERSON IN PAIN[80]

In the name of the Father and of the Son and of the Holy Spirit.
R Amen.

One of those present, or the minister, reads a text of sacred scripture, for example:

Brothers and sisters, listen to the holy gospel according to Luke 22:41-44:

Then he withdrew from them, about a stone's throw away, and knelt down and prayed. 'Father,' he said, 'if you are willing, take this cup away from me. Nevertheless, let your will be done, not mine.' Then an angel appeared to him, coming from heaven to give him strength. In his anguish he prayed even more earnestly, and his sweat fell to the ground like great drops of blood.

The minister introduces the intercessions:

Let us pray to God, the Father of mercy and compassion.

Another person present, or the minister, continues:

Your Son bore his agony in the garden and on the cross:
bless N., who now shares in his sufferings.
R Give us your blessing.

---

[80] Adapted from the *Book of Blessings*, n. 1984ff

Strengthen N. in his/her hour of need. R

Help us to be of service so that this burden of pain may be eased. R

The minister says the prayer of blessing:

Lord,
we, your people, pray for the gift of your holy blessing
to ward off every harm
and to bring to fulfilment every right desire.

Through Christ our Lord.
R Amen.

FOR A SITUATION OF POVERTY[81]

In the name of the Father and of the Son and of the Holy Spirit.
R Amen.

One of those present, or the minister, reads a text of sacred scripture, for example:

Brothers and sisters, listen to the holy gospel according to Matthew 6:25-29, 31-34:

That is why I am telling you not to worry about your life and what you are to eat, nor about your body and how you are to clothe it. Surely life means more than food, and the body more than clothing! Look at the birds in the sky. They do not sow or reap or gather into barns; yet your heavenly Father feeds them. Are you not worth much more than they are? Can any of you, for all his worrying, add one single cubit to his span of life? And why worry about clothing? Think of the flowers growing in the fields; they never have to work or spin; yet I assure you that not even Solomon in all his regalia was robed like one of these ... So do not worry, do not say, 'What are we to eat? What are we to drink? How are we to be clothed?' It is the pagans who set their hearts on these things. Your heavenly Father knows you need them all. Set your hearts on his kingdom first, and on righteousness, and all these other things will be given you as well. So do not worry about tomorrow:

---

[81] Adapted from the *Book of Blessings*, n. 1984ff

tomorrow will take care of itself. Each day has enough trouble of its own.

Or

Psalm 10:1-2:

Lord, why do you stand aside,
why hide from us now the times are hard?
The poor man is devoured by the pride of the wicked,
he is caught in the wiles that the other has devised.

The minister introduces the intercessions:

Let us ask the Lord to renew and support us with his strength.
R Lord, send us your blessing.

Another person present, or the minister, continues:

Look with kindness on us in our suffering. R

Ease our burdens and make our faith strong. R

May we have confidence and trust in your fatherly care. R

Protect our hearts from envy or bitterness. R

The minister concludes the rite by saying:

May God, who is blessed above all,
bless you in all things through Christ,
so that whatever happens in your lives
will work together for your good.
R Amen.

A priest or deacon continues:

And may almighty God bless you, the Father, and the
Son, ✠ and the Holy Spirit.
R Amen.

FOR RAIN[82]

In the name of the Father and of the Son and of the Holy Spirit.
R Amen.

One of those present, or the minister, reads a text of sacred scripture, for example:

Brothers and sisters, listen to the holy gospel according to Matthew 6:25-29, 31-34:

That is why I am telling you not to worry about your life and what you are to eat, nor about your body and how you are to clothe it. Surely life means more than food, and the body more than clothing! Look at the birds in the sky. They do not sow or reap or gather into barns; yet your heavenly Father feeds them. Are you not worth much more than they are? Can any of you, for all his worrying, add one single cubit to his span of life? And why worry about clothing? Think of the flowers growing in the fields; they never have to work or spin; yet I assure you that not even Solomon in all his regalia was robed like one of these … So do not worry, do not say, 'What are we to eat? What are we to drink? How are we to be clothed?' It is the pagans who set their hearts on these things. Your heavenly Father knows you need them all. Set your hearts on his kingdom first, and on righteousness, and all these other things will be given you as well. So do not worry about tomorrow:

---

[82] Adapted from the *Book of Blessings*, n. 1984ff

tomorrow will take care of itself. Each day has enough trouble of its own.

The minister introduces the intercessions:

God loves his creation and his goodness sustains the universe. Let us pray now that he will bless us and provide for our needs.
R Lord, send us your blessing.

Help us, O Lord, in our time of trouble. R

Send us the rain we need. R

Water the earth, giving growth and nourishment. R

Teach us to trust you and to seek your kingdom, finding in your love every good gift. R

The minister says the prayer of blessing:

Bless your people, Lord,
who wait for the gift of your compassion.
Grant that what they desire by your inspiration
they may receive through your goodness.

Through Christ our Lord.
R Amen.

The minister concludes the rite by saying:

May God, who is blessed above all,
bless you in all things through Christ,
so that whatever happens in your lives
will work together for your good.
R Amen.

A priest or deacon continues:

And may almighty God bless you, the Father, and the
Son, ✠ and the Holy Spirit.
R Amen.

FOR THOSE DISCERNING THEIR VOCATION[83]

In the name of the Father and of the Son and of the Holy Spirit.
R Amen.

One of those present, or the minister, reads a text of sacred scripture, for example:

Brothers and sisters, listen to the holy gospel according to Matthew 13:44-46:

Jesus said to his disciples:

'The kingdom of heaven is like treasure hidden in a field which someone has found; he hides it again, goes off happy, sells everything he owns and buys the field.

Again, the kingdom of heaven is like a merchant looking for fine pearls; when he finds one of great value he goes and sells everything he owns and buys it.'

The minister introduces the intercessions:

Let us pray to the Lord, who calls all people to himself.

Another person present, or the minister, continues:

Bless all who seek to discern the call of your love in their lives.
R Lord, send us your blessing.

---

[83] Adapted from the *Book of Blessings*, n. 1984ff

May your word, and the example of their brothers and sisters, be a light on their path. R

May the support of wise and faithful guides be a source of lasting encouragement. R

May the Holy Spirit give them light and courage. R

The minister says the prayer of blessing:

Lord,
we, your people, pray for the gift of your holy blessing
to ward off every harm
and to bring to fulfilment every right desire.
Through Christ our Lord.
R Amen.

The minister concludes the rite by saying:

May God, who is blessed above all,
bless you in all things through Christ,
so that whatever happens in your lives
will work together for your good.
R Amen.

A priest or deacon continues:

And may almighty God bless you, the Father, and the Son, ✠ and the Holy Spirit.
R Amen.

FOR PARENTS OF A SICK CHILD[84]

In the name of the Father and of the Son and of the Holy Spirit.
R Amen.

One of those present, or the minister, reads a text of sacred scripture, for example:

Brothers and sisters, listen to the holy gospel according to Luke 8:41, 50:

And now there came a man named Jairus, who was an official of the synagogue. He fell at Jesus' feet and pleaded with him to come to his house, because he had an only daughter about twelve years old, who was dying … 'Do not be afraid, only have faith and she will be saved.'

The minister introduces the intercessions:

Let us ask for the Lord's blessing on the parents of N. in their time of need.
R Lord, send us your blessing.

Another person, or the minister, continues:

May they find comfort in the love you have always shown to children. R

May they have courage as they care for N.. R

---

[84] Adapted from the *Book of Blessings*, n. 1984ff

May their faith be strengthened in moments of anguish or doubt. R

May they come closer to you and to one another in this time of illness. R

Bless your people, Lord,
who wait for the gift of your compassion.
Grant that what they desire by your inspiration
they may receive through your goodness.
Through Christ our Lord.
R Amen.

May God, who is blessed above all,
bless you in all things through Christ,
so that whatever happens in your lives
will work together for your good.
R Amen.

And may almighty God bless you, the Father, and the Son, ✠ and the Holy Spirit.
R Amen.

FOR TRAVELLING PEOPLE[85]

In the name of the Father and of the Son and of the Holy Spirit.
R Amen.

One of those present or the minister reads a text of sacred scripture, for example:

Brothers and sisters, listen to the words of the Book of Deuteronomy 26:5-9:

My father was a wandering Aramaean. He went down into Egypt to find refuge there, few in numbers; but there he became a nation, great, mighty, and strong. The Egyptians ill-treated us, they gave us no peace and inflicted harsh slavery on us. But we called on the Lord the God of our fathers. The Lord heard our voice and saw our misery, our toil and our oppression; and the Lord brought us out of Egypt with mighty hand and outstretched arm, with great terror, and with signs and wonders. He brought us here and gave us this land, a land where milk and honey flow.

The minister introduces the intercessions:

Let us pray to God, who loves us and sustains us.
R Lord, send us your blessing.

---

[85] Adapted from the *Book of Blessings*, n. 1984ff

Give your protection to all who are travellers in this land. R

May they find peace and acceptance. R

Protect them from illness and accidents. R

Give them wisdom and self-control. R

Give them courage and patience. R

The minister says the prayer of blessing:

Lord God,
from the abundance of your mercy
enrich your servants and safeguard them.
Strengthened by your blessing,
may they always be thankful to you
and bless you with unending joy.
Through Christ our Lord.
R Amen.

The minister concludes the rite by saying:

May God, who is blessed above all,
bless you in all things through Christ,
so that whatever happens in your lives
will work together for your good.
R Amen.

A priest or deacon continues:

And may almighty God bless you, the Father, and the
Son, ✠ and the Holy Spirit.
R Amen.

ADDITIONAL PRAYERS

PRAYER ON SATURDAY EVENING
FOR THE BEGINNING OF
THE LORD'S DAY

The celebration of the Lord's Day starts on Saturday evening. We celebrate the coming of the first day of the week: the day of the creation of light (Genesis 1:1-5); the day of the resurrection of Jesus (Luke 24:1-8); the day of the coming of the Spirit (Acts 2:1-27); the day of the gathering of the Christian community to celebrate the presence of the risen Jesus among the people gathered in his name (Matthew 18:20); in the proclamation of the word of scripture (Luke 24:25-32); and in the breaking of the Bread of Life (Luke 24:33-35). At the start of the Saturday evening meal or at another suitable time, one person may light a candle, while another prays the following, or a similar prayer, aloud:

This is the day which the Lord has made (Alleluia).
R Let us rejoice and be glad (Alleluia).

Let us pray:

Blessed are you, O Lord our God,
our Father, King of the universe;
you created light

in order to scatter the darkness of the world.
You raised Jesus, the light of the world,
in order to scatter the darkness of our lives.
You fill us with the Spirit of Jesus
so that we may live by his light.
We bless your holy name as we kindle this light (the candle is lit),
one of your many gifts to us.
Rekindle, we pray, the flame of the Holy Spirit
as we praise you for this day of the Lord.

Come, Lord Jesus (Alleluia).
R Do not delay (Alleluia).

One of the readings for Sunday Mass, or one of the readings referred to above, may be read, with a brief sharing, reflection or discussion.

SERENITY PRAYER

God, grant us the serenity to accept the things we cannot change, the courage to change the things we can, and the wisdom to know the difference. Amen.

PRAYER FOR PEACE

Jesus said:

'Peace I bequeath to you,
my own peace I give you,
a peace the world cannot give, this is my gift to you.
Do not let your hearts be troubled or afraid.' John
14:27

Let us pray.

Lord, God, our Father,
you seek the welfare of your children
and not their destruction: direct our wills towards the
peace for which we yearn;
and let there be peace among nations,
peace in our land,
peace in our homes,
and peace in our hearts,
that we may know that peace which passes all
understanding
in Jesus Christ our Lord.
R Amen.

God grant to the living, grace;
to the departed, rest;
to the Church, our country and all humanity, peace
and concord;
to us and to all his servants, life everlasting.
Through Christ our Lord.
R Amen.

PRAYER FOR A GATHERING OF MEN

In scripture we read that God formed man out of the dust of the ground, and breathed into his nostrils the breath of life, and man became a living soul.

Let us pray:

Lord God, you are the Lord and master of life.
It is your creative power moving within us that ultimately sustains us in existence.
Help us to realise that popularity, success, wealth and achievement will all pass away.
Help us, as men, to be able to acknowledge our weaknesses,
to be tender and kind to others
and to recognise you as our Lord and master.
Through Christ our Lord.

PRAYER FOR A GATHERING
OF WOMEN

'Yes, Lord,' Martha said, 'I believe that you are the Christ, the Son of God, the one who was to come into this world.'

When she had said this, she went and called her sister Mary, saying in a low voice, 'The Master is here and wants to see you.' John 11:27-28

Let us pray:

O Holy One, we thank and praise you for the wonder and mystery of womanhood.
We pray that the Christian Church may increasingly value the contribution which women can make to enrich the people of God.
We pray that Christian women today will proclaim their faith in Christ in all they do and say and, in so doing, will draw their sisters and brothers into a closer relationship with him and with one another.

May God grant them the confidence to stand up for what is right, the generosity which makes allowances for human frailty and the love which is always ready to go the second mile. We make this prayer through the one who invites us to follow him, Jesus Christ our Lord. Amen.

PRAYERS FOR THE DYING

These texts are not proposed as a substitute for either the sacrament of the sick or the celebration of viaticum. The sacrament of the sick should be celebrated at the beginning of a serious illness. Viaticum, celebrated when death is close, will then be better understood as the last sacrament of Christian life.[86] The texts given here are taken from a broader compendium of texts in the chapter in *Pastoral Care of the Sick* for Commendation of the Dying, which is understood as a help to sustain until death the union between the dying person and Christ which has been celebrated in viaticum.[87] A priest or deacon should be present at the Commendation of the Dying if possible.

Psalm 23
The Lord is my shepherd;
    I lack nothing.

In meadows of green grass he lets me lie.
To the waters of repose he leads me;
    there he revives my soul.

He guides me by paths of virtue
    for the sake of his name.

---

[86] *Pastoral Care of the Sick: Rites of Anointing and Viaticum.* English translation approved for use in the diocese of Ireland, England and Wales, Scotland, n. 175
[87] *Pastoral Care of the Sick,* n. 212

Though I pass through a gloomy valley,
    I fear no harm;
beside me your rod and your staff
    are there, to hearten me.

You prepare a table before me
    under the eyes of my enemies;
you anoint my head with oil,
    my cup brims over.

Ah, how goodness and kindness pursue me
    every day of my life;
my home, the house of the Lord,
    as long as I live!

Litany of the Saints

Holy Mary, Mother of God	pray for him/her
Holy angels of God	pray for him/her
Saint John the Baptist	pray for him/her
Saint Joseph	pray for him/her
Saint Peter and Saint Paul	pray for him/her

Other saints may be included here.

All holy men and women	pray for him/her

Prayer of Commendation, for use when the moment of death seems near:

Lord Jesus Christ, Saviour of the world,
we pray for your servant N.,
and commend him/her to your mercy.
For his/her sake you came down from heaven;
receive him/her now into the joy of your kingdom.

For though he/she has sinned,
he/she has not denied the Father, the Son and the
Holy Spirit,
but has believed in God and has worshipped his/her
Creator.
R Amen.

Prayer After Death
Loving and merciful God,
we entrust our brother/sister to your mercy.

You loved him/her greatly in this life:
now that he/she is freed from all its cares,
give him/her happiness and peace for ever.

The old order has passed away:
welcome him/her now into paradise
where there will be no more sorrow,
no more weeping or pain,
but only peace and joy
with Jesus, your Son,
and the Holy Spirit
for ever and ever.
R Amen.

For the solace of those present, a minister may
conclude these prayers with a simple blessing or with
a symbolic gesture, for example, signing the forehead
with the sign of the cross.

PRAYER FOR A HAPPY DEATH

May the Lord support us all day long, till the shades lengthen and the evening comes, the busy world is hushed, the fever of life is over and the work is done. Then in his mercy, may he give us a safe lodging, a holy rest and peace at the last.
Amen.

Cardinal John Henry Newman

PRAYERS FOR THE DEAD AND FOR THOSE WHO MOURN[88]

PRAYER AFTER DEATH

Holy Lord, almighty and eternal God,
hear our prayers for your servant N.,
whom you have summoned out of this world.
Forgive his/her sins and failings
and grant him/her a place of refreshment, light and peace.
Let him/her pass unharmed through the gates of death
to dwell with the blessed in light,
as you promised to Abraham and his children for ever.
Accept N. into your safekeeping
and on the great day of judgement
raise him/her up with all the saints
to inherit your eternal kingdom.
Through Christ our Lord.
R Amen.

GENERAL

God of loving kindness,
listen favourably to our prayers:
strengthen our belief that your Son has risen from the dead
and our hope that your servant N. will also rise again.
Through Christ our Lord.
R Amen.

---

[88] These prayers are taken from the *Order of Christian Funerals*.

A BAPTISED CHILD

Lord, in our grief we call upon your mercy:
open your ears to our prayers,
and one day unite us again with N.,
who, we firmly trust,
already enjoys eternal life in your kingdom.
Through Christ our Lord.
R Amen.

A CHILD WHO DIED BEFORE BAPTISM

O Lord, whose ways are beyond understanding,
listen to the prayers of your faithful people:
that those weighed down by grief
at the loss of this (little) child
may find reassurance in your infinite goodness.
Through Christ our Lord.
R Amen.

A STILLBORN CHILD

Lord God, ever caring and gentle, we commit to your love this little one, quickened to life for so short a time. Enfold him/her in eternal life.

We pray for his/her parents who are saddened by the loss of their baby.

Give them courage and help them in their pain and grief.

May they all meet one day in the joy and peace of your kingdom.

Through Christ our Lord.
R Amen.

A YOUNG PERSON
Lord,
your wisdom governs the length of our days.
We mourn the loss of N.,
whose life has passed so quickly,
and we entrust him/her to your mercy.
Welcome him/her into your heavenly dwelling
and grant him/her the happiness of everlasting youth.
Through Christ our Lord.
R Amen.

AN ELDERLY PERSON
God of endless ages,
from one generation to the next
you have been our refuge and strength.
Before the mountains were born
or the earth came to be,
you are God.
Have mercy now on your servant N.
whose long life was spent in your service.
Give him/her a place in your kingdom,
where hope is firm for all who love
and rest is sure for all who serve.
Through Christ our Lord.
R Amen.

ONE WHO DIED SUDDENLY
Lord,
as we mourn the sudden death of our brother/sister,
show us the immense power of your goodness
and strengthen our belief that N. has entered into your
presence.
Through Christ our Lord.
R Amen.

ONE WHO DIED BY SUICIDE
God, lover of souls,
you hold dear what you have made
and spare all things, for they are yours.
Look gently on your servant N.,
and by the blood of the cross
forgive his/her sins and failings.

Remember the faith of those who mourn
and satisfy their longing for that day
when all will be made new again
in Christ, our risen Lord,
who lives and reigns with you for ever and ever.
R Amen.

A TRADITIONAL PRAYER AT CHRISTMAS TIME

Céad failte romhat, a Linbh a gineadh sa Mhárta,
céad fáilte romhat, a Linbh a rugadh sa stábla.
Aoinmhic Mhuire, céad mile moladh leat,
is Dia bheatha do shláinte.

Word become flesh in the springtime, welcome indeed!
Child born in a winter stable, more than truly welcome!
Only Son of Mary, a hundred thousand praises be yours,
and may the blessed Lord of us all give you health!

FOR MISSING PERSONS

We read in the gospel how, as a child, Jesus remained in Jerusalem for three days without his parents' knowledge, leaving them worried and perplexed. When he was found, Mary his mother said to him, 'My child, why have you done this to us? See how worried your father and I have been, looking for you.' They did not understand the reply that Jesus gave, but he went down with them and came to Nazareth.

Let us pray:

God our Father,
your son Jesus Christ was restored to his loving family
after three days of absence and anxiety.
Watch over N., now missing, for whom we pray,
and protect him/her with your love.
Be near to those who are anxious for him/her;
let your presence change their sorrow into comfort,
their anxiety into trust,
their doubt into faith,
that they may know your loving purposes.
Through Christ our Lord.
R Amen.

FOR PRIESTS

We read in the gospel according to Matthew 9:35-37:

Jesus made a tour through all the towns and villages, teaching in their synagogues, proclaiming the Good News of the kingdom and curing all kinds of disease and sickness.

And when he saw the crowds he felt sorry for them because they were harassed and dejected, like sheep without a shepherd. Then he said to his disciples, 'The harvest is rich but the labourers are few, so ask the Lord of the harvest to send out labourers to his harvest.'

Let us pray for the Church and its leaders, especially for N..

Bless the pastors of your Church as faithful stewards and humble servants.
R Lord, send us your blessing.

Fill them with the fire of your love. R

May their ministry reveal your presence in the Church. R

May your power shine out through their weakness. R

Strengthen them in times of affliction and doubt. R

Comfort them when they are tempted or persecuted. R

Renew within them the gift of your Holy Spirit. R

Father, eternal Shepherd,
in Christ you gather us together
and lead us in the way of your commandments.
Hear our prayers for our brothers
who serve in the name of your Son:
fill them with every blessing,
and keep them faithful to him
who is Lord for ever and ever.
R Amen.

FOR PRISONERS

We read in St John's gospel:

Jesus said:

'If you make my word your home
you will indeed be my disciples,
you will learn the truth
and the truth will make you free …

I tell you most solemnly,
everyone who commits sin is a slave.
Now the slave's place in the house is not assured,
but the son's place is assured.
So if the Son makes you free,
you will be free indeed.' John 8:31-32, 34-36

Let us pray for N. (and N.)
and for all whose freedom has been taken away from them:
for all who suffer imprisonment, whether for crime or for the sake of conscience;
and for all whose vision of God's world is seen through bars.

God of mercy, bless N. (and N.).
R Lord, send us your blessing.

Give him/her/them courage and patience. R

Give him/her/them endurance in times of boredom and hardship. R

Give him/her/them tolerance towards others. R

Give him/her/them the possibility of an early release
and a new beginning in life. R

Our Father ...

May the Lord bless you and keep you.
R Amen.

May his face shine upon you,
and be gracious to you.
R Amen.

May he look upon you with kindness,
and give you his peace.
R Amen.

And may almighty God bless you, the Father, and the
Son, ✠ and the Holy Spirit.
R Amen.

A lay minister concludes by signing himself or herself
with the sign of the cross and saying:

May God, who is blessed above all,
bless us in all things through Christ,
so that whatever happens in our lives
will work together for our good.
R Amen.

FOR RELIGIOUS

In the gospel according to St John, Jesus says to his disciples:

'You did not choose me,
no, I chose you;
and I commissioned you
to go out and to bear fruit,
fruit that will last;
and then the Father will give you
anything you ask him in my name.
What command you
is to love one another.' John 15:16-17

May almighty God bless you
as you show to the world the immensity of divine love;
may Jesus Christ bless you
as you follow him in feeding the multitude who hunger
in body and soul;
may the Holy Spirit bless you
as you work for peace, unity and love among all
people.
And may the vows that bind you on earth
lead you to the community of eternal love
in the Holy Trinity for ever and ever.
R Amen.

FOR ONE WHO HAS LEFT RELIGIOUS LIFE

The vocation to live the gospel is given to everyone in the Church; the vocation to religious life is given only to some. In the gospel Jesus says to one: 'Go, sell all you possess and come follow me,' but to another he says: 'Go home to your family and tell them how much the Lord in his mercy has done for you.'

Let us pray.

Father of love and mercy,
bless the desire to follow Christ that is in N..
Reward the generous service already given to your people;
and find for him/her peace in your Church
and that happiness of living according to your perfect will.
Through Christ our Lord.
R Amen.

FOR TEACHERS OF THE YOUNG

Lord, pour out your Holy Spirit on N.,
privileged to work with the young.
May all his/her work with them
be marked by respect and sensitivity.
Teach him/her to show these young people their own
worth,
and to reveal your love for them.
Through his/her words and example
may he/she bring them closer to you.
Through Christ our Lord.
R Amen.

TRADITIONAL IRISH MEALTIME PRAYERS

Blessed by our Lord Jesus Christ
who shared the loaves and fishes with the five
thousand.
May the blessing of God be upon our meal
and upon our sharing in food and friendship.

Bless, O Lord, this food we are about to eat.
May it benefit us in body and soul.
As you, Lord, have shared your blessings with us,
may we be willing to share our food
with any creature in need this day.

All praise to the most generous God,
all praise to the King of heaven,
all praise to Jesus Christ
for the food that has refreshed us.
May he who has given us this food on earth,
grant us eternal food in heaven. Amen.

Unending thanks to you, all-powerful God, who have
given us these gifts.
May the God of heaven and his Son, Jesus Christ,
protect us against all who would do us any harm.
May he who gave us this food for the body
grant us a fine day,
a life without sin or shame,
the timely sacraments, a good death and eternal food
in heaven. Amen.

FOR LEADERS OF YOUTH CLUBS AND ACTIVITIES

Let us listen to the words of scripture from the gospel according to Matthew 18:1-4:

At this time the disciples came to Jesus and said, 'Who is the greatest in the kingdom of heaven?' So he called a little child to him and set the child in front of them. Then he said, 'I tell you solemnly, unless you change and become like little children you will never enter the kingdom of heaven. And so, the one who makes himself as little as this child is the greatest in the kingdom of heaven.'

Let us pray:

(That we will, like Jesus,
exercise leadership with service
and that, as his disciples,
we will care deeply for the young people entrusted to us.)

God, our Father,
We thank you for the joy and privilege
of working with and for our young people
who are so infinitely precious to you.
Help us, through the power of the Holy Spirit,
to exercise leadership with service,
and thus become more faithful disciples of Jesus your Son,
who is Lord for ever and ever. Amen.

INDEX OF BLESSINGS